Common Core Lessons

Text-Based Writing Nonfiction

Grade 3

The following photos were provided through Shutterstock.com and are protected by copyright:
Jim H Walling (page 14), bonchan (page 22), marco mayer (page 22), Francesco83 (page 22), Saiko3p (page 38), M. Unal Ozmen (page 38), Valentyn Volkov (page 38), Ronald Sumners (page 46), Marco Uliana (page 46), catwalker (page 54), Discovod (page 62), kojihirano (page 78), Digoarpi (page 86), ronstik (page 86), pjcross (page 86), Hung Chung Chih (page 94)

Remaining photos were provided by the organizations and individuals listed below and are also protected by copyright:
Library of Congress (page 54); NASA (page 118); Schalkwijk / Art Resource, NY; © 2013 Banco de México Diego Rivera Frida Kahlo Museums Trust, Mexico, D.F. / Artists Rights Society (ARS), New York (page 126)

Editorial Development: Renee Biermann
Cindie Farley
Lisa Vitarisi Mathews
Copy Editing: Cathy Harber
Art Direction: Cheryl Puckett
Art Management: Kathy Kopp
Cover Design: Yuki Meyer
Cover Illustration: Chris Vallo
Design/Production: Susan Lovell
Jessica Onken

EMC 6033

Evan-Moor.
Helping Children Learn

Visit
teaching-standards.com
to view a correlation
of this book.
This is a free service.

**Correlated to State and
Common Core State Standards**

**Congratulations on your purchase of some of the
finest teaching materials in the world.**

*Photocopying the pages in this book
is permitted for <u>single-classroom use only</u>.
Making photocopies for additional classes
or schools is prohibited.*

Contents

What's in Every Unit?

For the Teacher

Resource pages outline lesson objectives and provide instructional guidance.

The reading level helps identify appropriate texts.

Lesson objectives and content-area concepts are indicated.

Common Core State Standards correlations are located in each unit for easy reference.

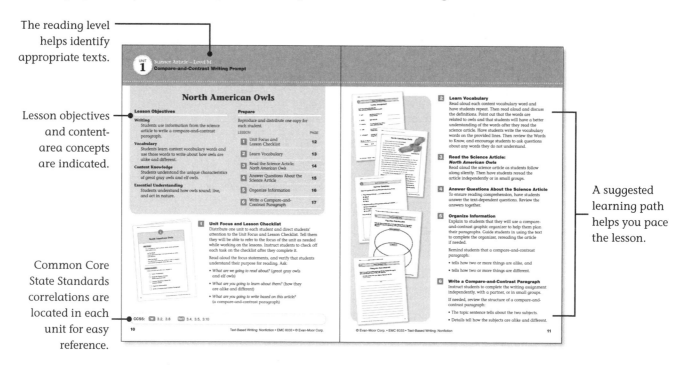

A suggested learning path helps you pace the lesson.

For the Student

Student pages provide unit focus, organizational tools, nonfiction content, and skills practice.

1 Unit Focus and Lesson Checklist

The Unit Focus provides a purpose for reading.

The Lesson Checklist guides students through the learning path.

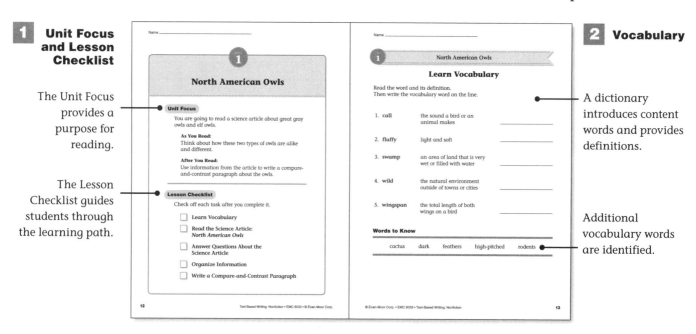

2 Vocabulary

A dictionary introduces content words and provides definitions.

Additional vocabulary words are identified.

3 **Nonfiction Article**

A short text introduces a content-area topic and provides details.

Illustrations and graphics provide additional information and context.

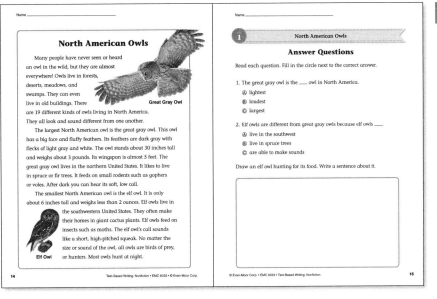

4 **Comprehension Questions**

Text-based questions appear in multiple-choice and constructed-response formats.

5 **Graphic Organizer**

A graphic organizer helps students organize information from the article to plan their writing.

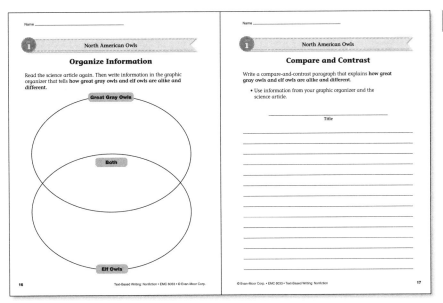

6 **Writing Prompt**

A text-based writing prompt helps students synthesize what they've learned.

Correlations:
Common Core State Standards

	Units							
	1	**2**	**3**	**4**	**5**	**6**	**7**	**8**
W Writing Standards for Grade 3	North American Owls	Melting Pot of Foods	Flowers and Insects	The Chocolate Process	The Venus' Flytrap	Charles Schulz	Pass the Salt	The Size of Asia
Text Types and Purposes								
3.1 Write opinion pieces on topics or texts, supporting a point of view with reasons. **a.** Introduce the topic or text they are writing about, state an opinion, and create an organizational structure that lists reasons. **b.** Provide reasons that support the opinion.								
3.2 Write informative/explanatory texts to examine a topic and convey ideas and information clearly. **b.** Develop the topic with facts, definitions, and details.	●	●	●	●	●	●	●	●
Research to Build and Present Knowledge								
3.8 Recall information from experiences or gather information from print and digital sources; take brief notes on sources and sort evidence into provided categories.	●	●	●	●	●	●	●	●
RIT Reading Standards for Informational Text, Grade 3								
Key Ideas and Details								
3.3 Describe the relationship between a series of historical events, scientific ideas or concepts, or steps in technical procedures in a text, using language that pertains to time, sequence, and cause/effect.		●	●	●	●	●	●	●
Craft and Structure								
3.4 Determine the meaning of general academic and domain-specific words and phrases in a text relevant to a grade 3 topic or subject area.	●	●	●	●	●	●	●	●
3.5 Use text features and search tools (e.g., key words, sidebars, hyperlinks) to locate information relevant to a given topic efficiently.	●	●	●	●	●	●	●	●
Range of Reading and Level of Text Complexity								
3.10 By the end of year, read and comprehend informational texts, including history/social studies, science, and technical texts, at the high end of the grades 2–3 text complexity band independently and proficiently.	●	●	●	●	●	●	●	●

Text-Based Writing: Nonfiction • EMC 6033 • © Evan-Moor Corp.

Units							W Writing Standards for Grade 3
9	10	11	12	13	14	15	
Birds Migrate	Weather Tools	We Need Sleep	Ancient Civilizations	Little Berry, Big Benefit	John Glenn	Mexico's Murals	
							Text Types and Purposes
			●	●	●	●	**3.1** Write opinion pieces on topics or texts, supporting a point of view with reasons. **a.** Introduce the topic or text they are writing about, state an opinion, and create an organizational structure that lists reasons. **b.** Provide reasons that support the opinion.
●	●	●					**3.2** Write informative/explanatory texts to examine a topic and convey ideas and information clearly. **b.** Develop the topic with facts, definitions, and details.
							Research to Build and Present Knowledge
●	●	●	●	●	●	●	**3.8** Recall information from experiences or gather information from print and digital sources; take brief notes on sources and sort evidence into provided categories.

							RIT **Reading Standards for Informational Text, Grade 3**
							Key Ideas and Details
●	●	●	●	●	●	●	**3.3** Describe the relationship between a series of historical events, scientific ideas or concepts, or steps in technical procedures in a text, using language that pertains to time, sequence, and cause/effect.
							Craft and Structure
●	●	●	●	●	●	●	**3.4** Determine the meaning of general academic and domain-specific words and phrases in a text relevant to a grade 3 topic or subject area.
●	●	●	●	●	●	●	**3.5** Use text features and search tools (e.g., key words, sidebars, hyperlinks) to locate information relevant to a given topic efficiently.
							Range of Reading and Level of Text Complexity
●	●	●	●	●	●	●	**3.10** By the end of year, read and comprehend informational texts, including history/social studies, science, and technical texts, at the high end of the grades 2–3 text complexity band independently and proficiently.

Correlations:
Texas Essential Knowledge and Skills

110.13 English Language Arts and Reading, Grade 3	Units				
	1	2	3	4	5
	North American Owls	Melting Pot of Foods	Flowers and Insects	The Chocolate Process	The Venus' Flytrap
Writing					
17) Writing/Writing Process. Students use elements of the writing process (planning, drafting, revising, editing, and publishing) to compose text. Students are expected to:	●	●	●	●	●
(A) plan a first draft by selecting a genre appropriate for conveying the intended meaning to an audience and generating ideas through a range of strategies (e.g., brainstorming, graphic organizers, logs, journals).	●	●	●	●	●
(20) Writing/Expository and Procedural Texts. Students write expository and procedural or work-related texts to communicate ideas and information to specific audiences for specific purposes. Students are expected to:	●	●	●	●	●
(C) write responses to literary or expository texts that demonstrate an understanding of the text.	●	●	●	●	●
(21) Writing/Persuasive Texts. Students write persuasive texts to influence the attitudes or actions of a specific audience on specific issues. Students are expected to write persuasive essays for appropriate audiences that establish a position and use supporting details.					
Reading					
(13) Reading/Comprehension of Informational Text/ Expository Text. Students analyze, make inferences, and draw conclusions about expository text and provide evidence from text to support their understanding. Students are expected to:	●	●	●	●	●
(B) draw conclusions from the facts presented in text and support those assertions with textual evidence;	●	●	●	●	●
(C) identify explicit cause-and-effect relationships among ideas in texts; and					
(D) use text features (e.g., bold print, captions, key words, italics) to locate information and make and verify predictions about contents of text.	●	●	●	●	●
(15) Reading/Comprehension of Informational Text/ Procedural Texts. Students understand how to glean and use information in procedural texts and documents. Students are expected to:	●	●	●		●
(A) follow and explain a set of written multi-step directions; and			●	●	●
(B) locate and use specific information in graphic features of text.	●	●		●	●

Units									
6	7	8	9	10	11	12	13	14	15
Charles Schulz	Pass the Salt	The Size of Asia	Birds Migrate	Weather Tools	We Need Sleep	Ancient Civilizations	Little Berry, Big Benefit	John Glenn	Mexico's Murals
•	•	•	•	•	•	•	•	•	•
•	•	•	•	•	•	•	•	•	•
•	•	•		•	•				
•	•	•	•	•	•	•	•	•	•
						•	•	•	•
•	•	•	•	•	•	•	•	•	•
•	•	•	•	•	•	•	•	•	•
			•	•	•				
•	•	•	•	•	•	•	•	•	•
•	•	•	•	•	•	•	•	•	•
•	•								
		•	•	•			•		•

North American Owls

Lesson Objectives

Writing
Students use information from the science article to write a compare-and-contrast paragraph.

Vocabulary
Students learn content vocabulary words and use those words to write about how owls are alike and different.

Content Knowledge
Students understand the unique characteristics of great gray owls and elf owls.

Essential Understanding
Students understand how owls sound, live, and act in nature.

Prepare

Reproduce and distribute one copy for each student.

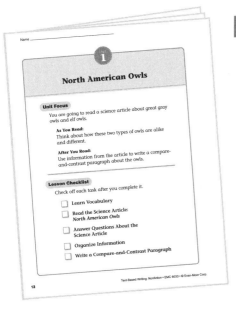

1 Unit Focus and Lesson Checklist

Distribute one unit to each student and direct students' attention to the Unit Focus and Lesson Checklist. Tell them they will be able to refer to the focus of the unit as needed while working on the lessons. Instruct students to check off each task on the checklist after they complete it.

Read aloud the focus statements, and verify that students understand their purpose for reading. Ask:

- *What are we going to read about?* (great gray owls and elf owls)

- *What are you going to learn about them?* (how they are alike and different)

- *What are you going to write based on this article?* (a compare-and-contrast paragraph)

CCSS: **W** 3.2, 3.8 **RIT** 3.4, 3.5, 3.10

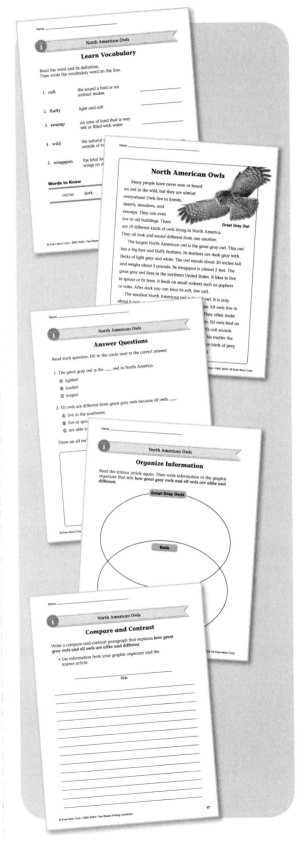

2 Learn Vocabulary

Read aloud each content vocabulary word and have students repeat. Then read aloud and discuss the definitions. Point out that the words are related to owls and that students will have a better understanding of the words after they read the science article. Have students write the vocabulary words on the provided lines. Then review the Words to Know, and encourage students to ask questions about any words they do not understand.

3 Read the Science Article: *North American Owls*

Read aloud the science article as students follow along silently. Then have students reread the article independently or in small groups.

4 Answer Questions About the Science Article

To ensure reading comprehension, have students answer the text-dependent questions. Review the answers together.

5 Organize Information

Explain to students that they will use a compare-and-contrast graphic organizer to help them plan their paragraphs. Guide students in using the text to complete the organizer, rereading the article if needed.

Remind students that a compare-and-contrast paragraph:

• tells how two or more things are alike, and

• tells how two or more things are different.

6 Write a Compare-and-Contrast Paragraph

Instruct students to complete the writing assignment independently, with a partner, or in small groups.

If needed, review the structure of a compare-and-contrast paragraph:

• The topic sentence tells about the two subjects.

• Details tell how the subjects are alike and different.

UNIT
1

North American Owls

Unit Focus

You are going to read a science article about great gray owls and elf owls.

As You Read:

Think about how these two types of owls are alike and different.

After You Read:

Use information from the article to write a compare-and-contrast paragraph about the owls.

Lesson Checklist

Check off each task after you complete it.

- [ ] **Learn Vocabulary**

- [ ] **Read the Science Article:** *North American Owls*

- [ ] **Answer Questions About the Science Article**

- [ ] **Organize Information**

- [ ] **Write a Compare-and-Contrast Paragraph**

Text-Based Writing: Nonfiction • EMC 6033 • © Evan-Moor Corp.

North American Owls

Learn Vocabulary

Read the word and its definition.
Then write the vocabulary word on the line.

1. **call**   the sound a bird or an animal makes   _____

2. **fluffy**   light and soft   _____

3. **swamp**   an area of land that is very wet or filled with water   _____

4. **wild**   the natural environment outside of towns or cities   _____

5. **wingspan**   the total length of both wings on a bird   _____

Words to Know

cactus	dark	feathers	high-pitched	rodents

North American Owls

Many people have never seen or heard an owl in the wild, but they are almost everywhere! Owls live in forests, deserts, meadows, and swamps. They can even live in old buildings. There

Great Gray Owl

are 19 different kinds of owls living in North America. They all look and sound different from one another.

The largest North American owl is the great gray owl. This owl has a big face and fluffy feathers. Its feathers are dark gray with flecks of light gray and white. The owl stands about 30 inches tall and weighs about 3 pounds. Its wingspan is almost 5 feet. The great gray owl lives in the northern United States. It likes to live in spruce or fir trees. It feeds on small rodents such as gophers or voles. After dark you can hear its soft, low call.

The smallest North American owl is the elf owl. It is only about 6 inches tall and weighs less than 2 ounces. Elf owls live in

Elf Owl

the southwestern United States. They often make their homes in giant cactus plants. Elf owls feed on insects such as moths. The elf owl's call sounds like a short, high-pitched squeak. No matter the size or sound of the owl, all owls are birds of prey, or hunters. Most owls hunt at night.

UNIT 1

North American Owls

Answer Questions

Read each question. Fill in the circle next to the correct answer.

1. The great gray owl is the ___ owl in North America.

    Ⓐ lightest

    Ⓑ loudest

    Ⓒ largest

2. Elf owls are different from great gray owls because elf owls ___.

    Ⓐ live in the southwest

    Ⓑ live in spruce trees

    Ⓒ are able to make sounds

Draw an elf owl hunting for its food. Write a sentence about it.

North American Owls

Organize Information

Read the science article again. Then write information in the graphic organizer that tells **how great gray owls and elf owls are alike and different.**

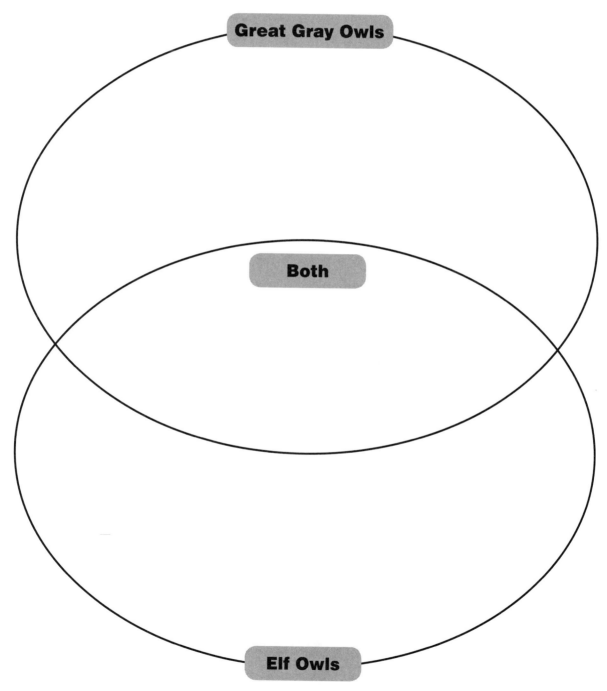

Great Gray Owls

Both

Elf Owls

Name _____

Compare and Contrast

Write a compare-and-contrast paragraph that explains **how great gray owls and elf owls are alike and different**.

- Use information from your graphic organizer and the science article.

_____
Title

_____

_____

_____

_____

_____

_____

_____

_____

_____

_____

_____

_____

Melting Pot of Foods

Lesson Objectives

Writing
Students use information from the health article to write a compare-and-contrast paragraph.

Vocabulary
Students learn content vocabulary words and use those words to write about how two traditional meals are alike and different.

Content Knowledge
Students learn the ingredients and health benefits of three traditional meals.

Essential Understanding
Students understand that we all benefit from eating foods from other countries or cultures.

Prepare the Unit

Reproduce and distribute one copy for each student.

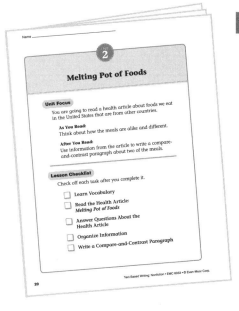

1 Unit Focus and Lesson Checklist

Distribute one unit to each student and direct students' attention to the Unit Focus and Lesson Checklist. Tell them they will be able to refer to the focus of the unit as needed while working on the lessons. Instruct students to check off each task on the checklist after they complete it.

Read aloud the focus statements, and verify that students understand their purpose for reading. Ask:

- *What are we going to read about?* (foods we eat in the United States that are from other countries)

- *What are you going to learn about them?* (how they are alike and different)

- *What are you going to write based on this article?* (a compare-and-contrast paragraph)

CCSS: 3.2, 3.8   3.3, 3.4, 3.5, 3.10

Text-Based Writing: Nonfiction • EMC 6033 • © Evan-Moor Corp.

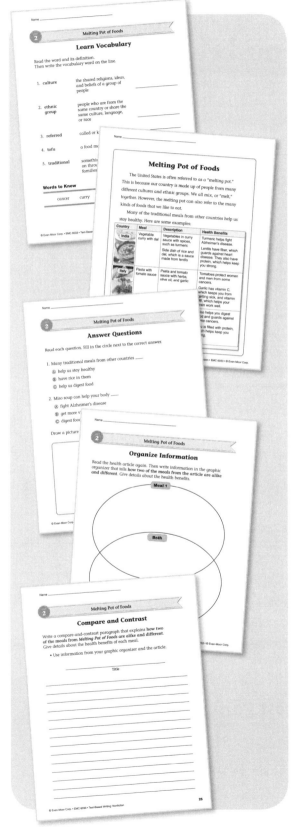

2 Learn Vocabulary

Read aloud each content vocabulary word and have students repeat. Then read aloud and discuss the definitions. Point out that the words are related to traditional meals and that students will have a better understanding of the words after they read the health article. Have students write the vocabulary words on the provided lines. Then review the Words to Know, and encourage students to ask questions about any words they do not understand.

3 Read the Health Article: *Melting Pot of Foods*

Read aloud the health article as students follow along silently. Then have students reread the article independently or in small groups.

4 Answer Questions About the Health Article

To ensure reading comprehension, have students answer the text-dependent questions. Review the answers together.

5 Organize Information

Explain to students that they will use a compare-and-contrast graphic organizer to help them plan their paragraphs. Guide students in using the text to complete the organizer, rereading the article if needed.

Remind students that a compare-and-contrast paragraph:

• tells how two or more things are alike, and

• tells how two or more things are different.

6 Write a Compare-and-Contrast Paragraph

Have students complete the writing assignment independently, with a partner, or in small groups.

Review the structure of a compare-and-contrast paragraph:

• The topic sentence tells about the two subjects.

• Details tell how the subjects are alike and different.

UNIT 2

Melting Pot of Foods

Unit Focus

You are going to read a health article about foods we eat in the United States that are from other countries.

As You Read:

Think about how the meals are alike and different.

After You Read:

Use information from the article to write a compare-and-contrast paragraph about two of the meals.

Lesson Checklist

Check off each task after you complete it.

☐ **Learn Vocabulary**

☐ **Read the Health Article:** *Melting Pot of Foods*

☐ **Answer Questions About the Health Article**

☐ **Organize Information**

☐ **Write a Compare-and-Contrast Paragraph**

Name _____

Learn Vocabulary

Read the word and its definition.
Then write the vocabulary word on the line.

1. **culture**   the shared religions, ideas, and beliefs of a group of people

_____

2. **ethnic group**   people who are from the same country or share the same culture, language, or race

_____

3. **referred**   called or known as

_____

4. **tofu**   a food made from soybeans

_____

5. **traditional**   something that is passed on through generations of families or groups

_____

Words to Know

cancer	curry	guard	heart disease	vitamin

Melting Pot of Foods

The United States is often referred to as a "melting pot." This is because our country is made up of people from many different cultures and ethnic groups. We all mix, or "melt," together. However, the melting pot can also refer to the many kinds of foods that we like to eat.

Many of the traditional meals from other countries help us stay healthy. Here are some examples:

Country	Meal	Description	Health Benefits
India	Vegetable curry with dal	Vegetables in curry sauce with spices, such as turmeric Side dish of rice and dal, which is a sauce made from lentils	Turmeric helps fight Alzheimer's disease. Lentils have fiber, which guards against heart disease. They also have protein, which helps keep you strong.
Italy	Pasta with tomato sauce	Pasta and tomato sauce with herbs, olive oil, and garlic	Tomatoes protect women and men from some cancers. Garlic has vitamin C, which keeps you from getting sick, and vitamin B6, which helps your brain work well.
Japan	Miso soup	Miso is soybean paste mixed with water. It's served with seaweed, green onions, and tofu.	Miso helps you digest food and guards against some cancers. Tofu is filled with protein, which helps keep you strong.

Text-Based Writing: Nonfiction • EMC 6033 • © Evan-Moor Corp.

Melting Pot of Foods

Answer Questions

Read each question. Fill in the circle next to the correct answer.

1. Many traditional meals from other countries ____.

   Ⓐ help us stay healthy

   Ⓑ have rice in them

   Ⓒ help us digest food

2. Miso soup can help your body ____.

   Ⓐ fight Alzheimer's disease

   Ⓑ get more vitamin C

   Ⓒ digest food more easily

Draw a picture of a healthful food that you eat. Write a sentence about it.

Name _____

Organize Information

Read the health article again. Then write information in the graphic organizer that tells **how two of the meals from the article are alike and different**. Give details about the health benefits.

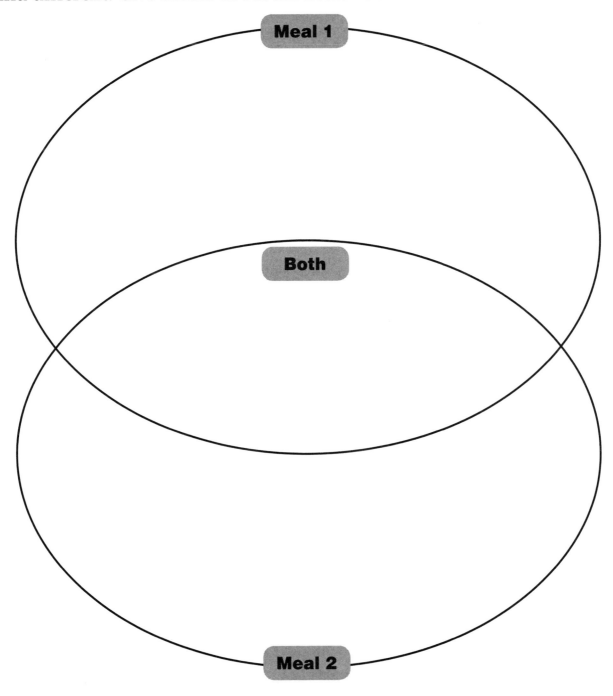

Meal 1

Both

Meal 2

Name _____

Compare and Contrast

Write a compare-and-contrast paragraph that explains **how two of the meals from *Melting Pot of Foods* are alike and different.** Give details about the health benefits of each meal.

- Use information from your graphic organizer and the article.

_____
Title

_____

_____

_____

_____

_____

_____

_____

_____

_____

_____

Flowers and Insects

Lesson Objectives

Writing
Students use information from the science article to write a sequence paragraph.

Vocabulary
Students learn content vocabulary words and use those words to write about plant reproduction.

Content Knowledge
Students understand that insects and birds carry pollen to and from flowers.

Essential Understanding
Students understand that plants, insects, and birds work together to survive.

Prepare

Reproduce and distribute one copy for each student.

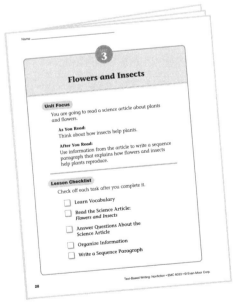

1 **Unit Focus and Lesson Checklist**

Distribute one unit to each student and direct students' attention to the Unit Focus and Lesson Checklist. Tell them they will be able to refer to the focus of the unit as needed while working on the lessons. Instruct students to check off each task on the checklist after they complete it.

Read aloud the focus statements, and verify that students understand their purpose for reading. Ask:

• *What are we going to read about?* (plants and flowers)

• *What are you going to learn about them?* (how insects help plants)

• *What are you going to write based on this article?* (a sequence paragraph)

CCSS: 3.2, 3.8   3.3, 3.4, 3.5, 3.10

Text-Based Writing: Nonfiction • EMC 6033 • © Evan-Moor Corp.

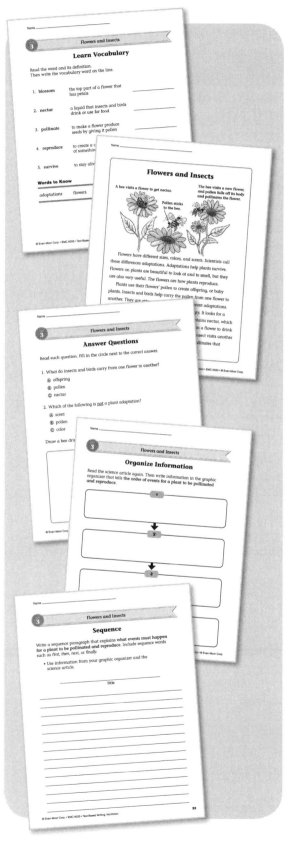

2 Learn Vocabulary

Read aloud each content vocabulary word and have students repeat. Then read aloud and discuss the definitions. Point out that the words are related to plants and that students will have a better understanding of the words after they read the science article. Have students write the vocabulary words on the provided lines. Then review the Words to Know, and encourage students to ask questions about any words they do not understand.

3 Read the Science Article: *Flowers and Insects*

Read aloud the science article as students follow along silently. Then have students reread the article independently or in small groups.

4 Answer Questions About the Science Article

To ensure reading comprehension, have students answer the text-dependent questions. Review the answers together.

5 Organize Information

Explain to students that they will use a sequence graphic organizer to help them plan their paragraphs. Guide students in using the text to complete the organizer, rereading the article if needed.

Remind students that a sequence paragraph:

- tells the time order of events, and

- allows readers to understand exactly how a process works.

6 Write a Sequence Paragraph

Instruct students to complete the writing assignment independently, with a partner, or in small groups.

If needed, review the structure of a sequence paragraph:

- The topic sentence tells the subject of the paragraph.

- Detail sentences list the events in order.

UNIT 3

Flowers and Insects

Unit Focus

You are going to read a science article about plants and flowers.

As You Read:

Think about how insects help plants.

After You Read:

Use information from the article to write a sequence paragraph that explains how flowers and insects help plants reproduce.

Lesson Checklist

Check off each task after you complete it.

☐ Learn Vocabulary

☐ Read the Science Article:
Flowers and Insects

☐ Answer Questions About the
Science Article

☐ Organize Information

☐ Write a Sequence Paragraph

Learn Vocabulary

Read the word and its definition.
Then write the vocabulary word on the line.

1. **blossom**   the top part of a flower that
                    has petals   _____

2. **nectar**   a liquid that insects and birds
                    drink or use for food   _____

3. **pollinate**   to make a flower produce
                    seeds by giving it pollen   _____

4. **reproduce**   to create a copy or a new form
                    of something   _____

5. **survive**   to stay alive   _____

Words to Know

adaptations   flowers   offspring   plants   pollen   scents

Flowers and Insects

A bee visits a flower to get nectar.

The bee visits a new flower, and pollen falls off its body and pollinates the flower.

Pollen sticks to the bee.

Flowers have different sizes, colors, and scents. Scientists call these differences adaptations. Adaptations help plants survive. Flowers on plants are beautiful to look at and to smell, but they are also very useful. The flowers are how plants reproduce.

Plants use their flowers' pollen to create offspring, or baby plants. Insects and birds help carry the pollen from one flower to another. They are attracted to the flowers' different adaptations.

The process starts when an insect gets hungry. It looks for a pretty or sweet-smelling blossom. The flower contains nectar, which is a sweet, sugary liquid. When an insect lands on a flower to drink the nectar, pollen sticks to the insect. When the insect visits another flower, some of the pollen falls off its body and pollinates that flower. Now, a new plant will grow!

Name _____

Answer Questions

Read each question. Fill in the circle next to the correct answer.

1. What do insects and birds carry from one flower to another?

   Ⓐ offspring

   Ⓑ pollen

   Ⓒ nectar

2. Which of the following is <u>not</u> a plant adaptation?

   Ⓐ scent

   Ⓑ pollen

   Ⓒ color

Draw a bee drinking nectar from a flower.

UNIT
3

Organize Information

Read the science article again. Then write information in the graphic organizer that tells **the order of events for a plant to be pollinated and reproduce.**

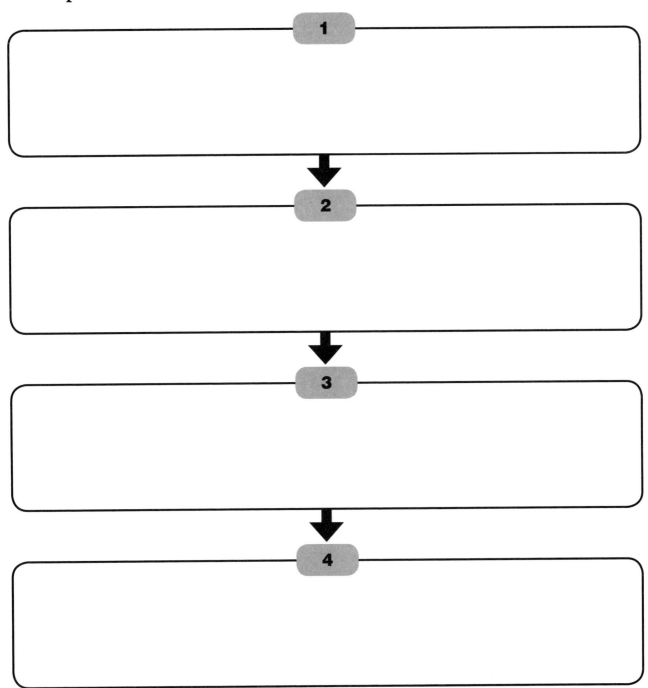

1

2

3

4

Name _____

Sequence

Write a sequence paragraph that explains **what events must happen for a plant to be pollinated and reproduce.** Include sequence words such as *first, then, next,* or *finally.*

- Use information from your graphic organizer and the science article.

_____
Title

_____

_____

_____

_____

_____

_____

_____

_____

_____

_____

_____

_____

The Chocolate Process

Lesson Objectives

Writing
Students use information from the science article to write a sequence paragraph.

Vocabulary
Students learn content vocabulary words and use those words to write about chocolate.

Content Knowledge
Students understand that chocolate comes from cacao tree pods.

Essential Understanding
Students understand that many steps are involved to take food products from the farm and produce the final product.

Prepare

Reproduce and distribute one copy for each student.

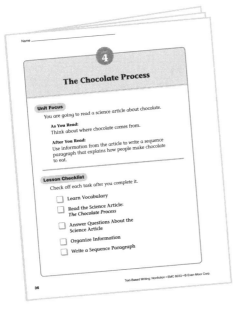

1 Unit Focus and Lesson Checklist

Distribute one unit to each student and direct students' attention to the Unit Focus and Lesson Checklist. Tell them they will be able to refer to the focus of the unit as needed while working on the lessons. Instruct students to check off each task on the checklist after they complete it.

Read aloud the focus statements, and verify that students understand their purpose for reading. Ask:

• *What are we going to read about?* (chocolate)

• *What are you going to learn about it?* (where it comes from)

• *What are you going to write based on this article?* (a sequence paragraph)

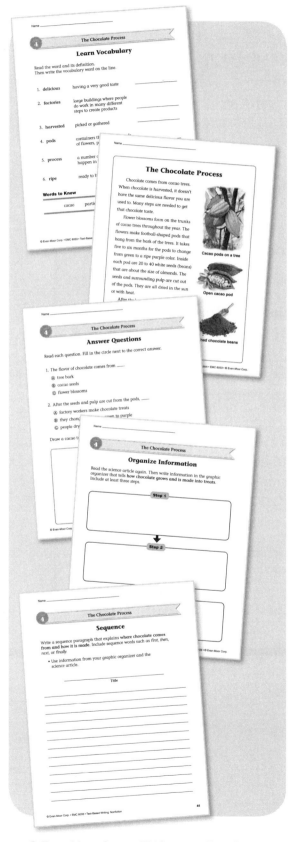

2 Learn Vocabulary

Read aloud each content vocabulary word and have students repeat. Then read aloud and discuss the definitions. Point out that the words are related to chocolate and that students will have a better understanding of the words after they read the science article. Have students write the vocabulary words on the provided lines. Then review the Words to Know, and encourage students to ask questions about any words they do not understand.

3 Read the Science Article: *The Chocolate Process*

Read aloud the science article as students follow along silently. Then have students reread the article independently or in small groups.

4 Answer Questions About the Science Article

To ensure reading comprehension, have students answer the text-dependent questions. Review the answers together.

5 Organize Information

Explain to students that they will use a sequence graphic organizer to help them plan their paragraphs. Guide students in using the text to complete the organizer, rereading the article if needed.

Remind students that a sequence paragraph:

- tells the chronological order, or time order, of events, and

- allows readers to understand exactly how a process works.

6 Write a Sequence Paragraph

Instruct students to complete the writing assignment independently, with a partner, or in small groups.

If needed, review the structure of a sequence paragraph:

- The topic sentence tells the subject.

- Detail sentences support the topic sentence and list the events or steps in order.

The Chocolate Process

Unit Focus

You are going to read a science article about chocolate.

As You Read:
Think about where chocolate comes from.

After You Read:
Use information from the article to write a sequence paragraph that explains how people make chocolate to eat.

Lesson Checklist

Check off each task after you complete it.

☐ **Learn Vocabulary**

☐ **Read the Science Article:** *The Chocolate Process*

☐ **Answer Questions About the Science Article**

☐ **Organize Information**

☐ **Write a Sequence Paragraph**

Name _____

Learn Vocabulary

Read the word and its definition.
Then write the vocabulary word on the line.

1. **delicious**   having a very good taste   _____

2. **factories**   large buildings where people do work in many different steps to create products   _____

3. **harvested**   picked or gathered   _____

4. **pods**   containers that hold the seeds of flowers, plants, or trees   _____

5. **process**   a number of changes that happen in a certain order   _____

6. **ripe**   ready to be safely eaten   _____

Words to Know

cacao   particles   pulp   roasted   treats

The Chocolate Process

Chocolate comes from cacao trees. When chocolate is harvested, it doesn't have the same delicious flavor you are used to. Many steps are needed to get that chocolate taste.

Flower blossoms form on the trunks of cacao trees throughout the year. The flowers make football-shaped pods that hang from the bark of the trees. It takes five to six months for the pods to change from green to a ripe purple color. Inside each pod are 20 to 40 white seeds (beans) that are about the size of almonds. The seeds and surrounding pulp are cut out of the pods. They are all dried in the sun or with heat.

After the beans are thoroughly dried, they turn a dark chocolate color and are shipped to candy factories all over the world. In the factories, chocolate beans are brushed clean, roasted, and crushed into particles. Now the chocolate is ready to be made into delicious chocolate treats!

Cacao pods on a tree

Open cacao pod

Crushed chocolate beans

UNIT
4

The Chocolate Process

Answer Questions

Read each question. Fill in the circle next to the correct answer.

1. The flavor of chocolate comes from ____.

   Ⓐ tree bark

   Ⓑ cacao seeds

   Ⓒ flower blossoms

2. After the seeds and pulp are cut from the pods, ____.

   Ⓐ factory workers make chocolate treats

   Ⓑ they change color from green to purple

   Ⓒ people dry them with heat or in the sun

Draw a cacao tree that is ready to be harvested.

Name _____

Organize Information

Read the science article again. Then write information in the graphic organizer that tells **how chocolate grows and is made into treats.** Include at least three steps.

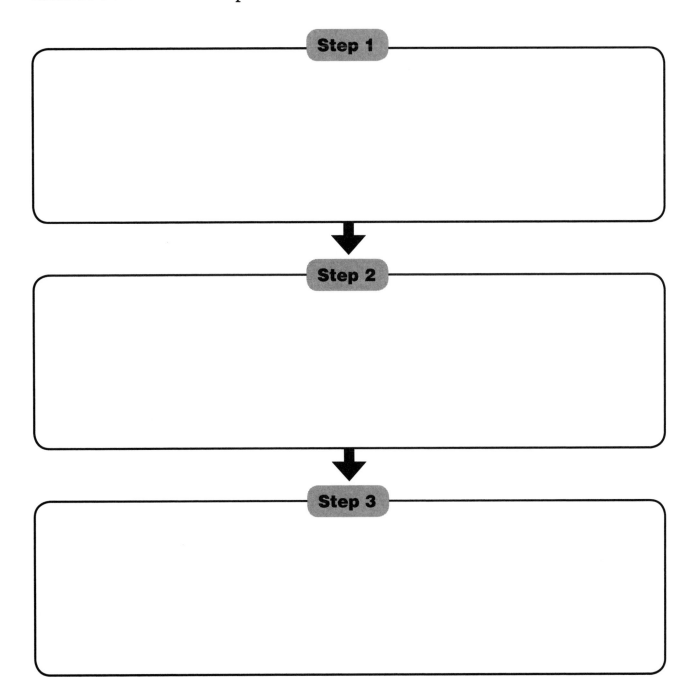

Step 1

Step 2

Step 3

Name _____

The Chocolate Process

Sequence

Write a sequence paragraph that explains **where chocolate comes from and how it is made**. Include sequence words such as *first, then, next,* or *finally.*

- Use information from your graphic organizer and the science article.

_____

Title

_____

_____

_____

_____

_____

_____

_____

_____

_____

_____

_____

_____

The Venus' Flytrap

Lesson Objectives

Writing
Students use information from the science article to write a sequence paragraph.

Vocabulary
Students learn content vocabulary words and use those words to write about Venus' flytraps.

Content Knowledge
Students understand that there is a sequence Venus' flytraps use to catch and digest food.

Essential Understanding
Students understand that some plants rely on more than just soil, sunlight, and water to stay alive.

Prepare

Reproduce and distribute one copy for each student.

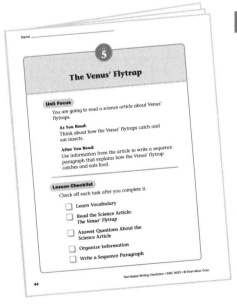

1 Unit Focus and Lesson Checklist

Distribute one unit to each student and direct students' attention to the Unit Focus and Lesson Checklist. Tell them they will be able to refer to the focus of the unit as needed while working on the lessons. Instruct students to check off each task on the checklist after they complete it.

Read aloud the focus statements, and verify that students understand their purpose for reading. Ask:

- *What are we going to read about?* (Venus' flytraps)

- *What are you going to learn about them?* (how they catch and eat insects)

- *What are you going to write based on this article?* (a sequence paragraph)

CCSS: 3.2, 3.8   3.3, 3.4, 3.5, 3.10

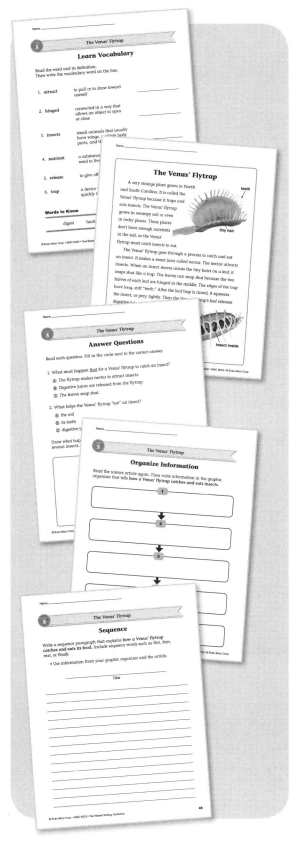

2   Learn Vocabulary

Read aloud each content vocabulary word and have students repeat. Then read aloud and discuss the definitions. Point out that the words are related to Venus' flytraps and that students will have a better understanding of the words after they read the science article. Have students write the vocabulary words on the provided lines. Then review the Words to Know, and encourage students to ask questions about any words they do not understand.

3   Read the Science Article: *The Venus' Flytrap*

Read aloud the science article as students follow along silently. Then have students reread the article independently or in small groups.

4   Answer Questions About the Science Article

To ensure reading comprehension, have students answer the text-dependent questions. Review the answers together.

5   Organize Information

Explain to students that they will use a sequence graphic organizer to help them plan their paragraphs. Guide students in using the text to complete the organizer, rereading the article if needed.

Remind students that a sequence paragraph:

- tells the chronological order, or time order, of events, and

- allows readers to understand exactly how a process works.

6   Write a Sequence Paragraph

Instruct students to complete the writing assignment independently, with a partner, or in small groups.

If needed, review the structure of a sequence paragraph:

- The topic sentence tells the subject of the paragraph.

- Detail sentences support the topic sentence and list the events in order.

UNIT 5

The Venus' Flytrap

Unit Focus

You are going to read a science article about Venus' flytraps.

As You Read:

Think about how the Venus' flytraps catch and eat insects.

After You Read:

Use information from the article to write a sequence paragraph that explains how the Venus' flytrap catches and eats food.

Lesson Checklist

Check off each task after you complete it.

- [ ] **Learn Vocabulary**
- [ ] **Read the Science Article:** *The Venus' Flytrap*
- [ ] **Answer Questions About the Science Article**
- [ ] **Organize Information**
- [ ] **Write a Sequence Paragraph**

Name _____

Learn Vocabulary

Read the word and its definition.
Then write the vocabulary word on the line.

1. **attract**   to pull or to draw toward oneself   _____

2. **hinged**   connected in a way that allows an object to open or close   _____

3. **insects**   small animals that usually have wings, multiple body parts, and three pairs of legs   _____

4. **nutrient**   a substance that living things need to live and grow   _____

5. **release**   to give off; to let go of   _____

6. **trap**   a device that snaps closed quickly to catch animals   _____

Words to Know

digest   hunting   prey   process   strange

The Venus' Flytrap

A very strange plant grows in North and South Carolina. It is called the Venus' flytrap because it traps and eats insects. The Venus' flytrap grows in swampy soil or even in rocky places. These places don't have enough nutrients in the soil, so the Venus' flytrap must catch insects to eat.

teeth

tiny hair

The Venus' flytrap goes through a process to catch and eat an insect. It makes a sweet juice called nectar. The nectar attracts insects. When an insect moves across the tiny hairs on a leaf, it snaps shut like a trap. The leaves can snap shut because the two halves of each leaf are hinged in the middle. The edges of the trap have long, stiff "teeth." After the leaf trap is closed, it squeezes the insect, or prey, tightly. Then the Venus' flytrap's leaf releases digestive juices. These juices help the plant "eat," or digest, the insect. After a leaf has trapped several insects, it dies. Then a new leaf grows to start hunting again!

insect inside

Name _____

UNIT
5

The Venus' Flytrap

Answer Questions

Read each question. Fill in the circle next to the correct answer.

1. What must happen <u>first</u> for a Venus' flytrap to catch an insect?

Ⓐ The flytrap makes nectar to attract insects.

Ⓑ Digestive juices are released from the flytrap.

Ⓒ The leaves snap shut.

2. What helps the Venus' flytrap "eat" an insect?

Ⓐ the soil

Ⓑ its teeth

Ⓒ digestive juices

Draw what happens to a Venus' flytrap after its leaf has eaten several insects.

Organize Information

Read the science article again. Then write information in the graphic organizer that tells **how a Venus' flytrap catches and eats insects.**

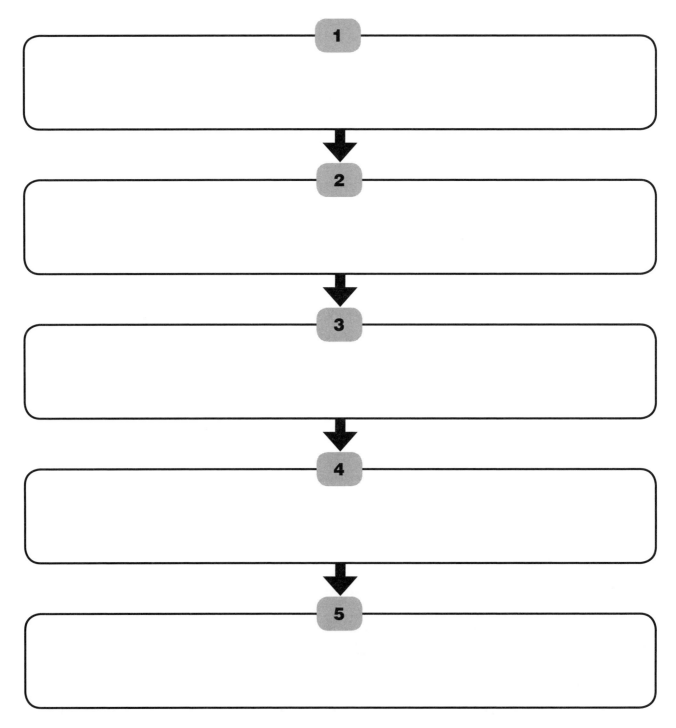

Name _____

Sequence

Write a sequence paragraph that explains **how a Venus' flytrap catches and eats its food**. Include sequence words such as *first*, *then*, *next*, or *finally*.

- Use information from your graphic organizer and the article.

_____
Title

_____

_____

_____

_____

_____

_____

_____

_____

_____

_____

_____

Charles Schulz

Lesson Objectives

Writing
Students use information from the biography to write a sequence paragraph.

Vocabulary
Students learn content vocabulary words and use those words to write about Charles Schulz.

Content Knowledge
Students understand that Charles Schulz created *Peanuts* and Charlie Brown.

Essential Understanding
Students understand that Charles Schulz worked hard during his lifetime and is a famous cartoonist even today.

Prepare

Reproduce and distribute one copy for each student.

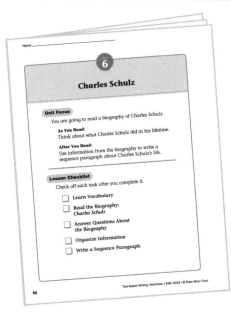

1 Unit Focus and Lesson Checklist

Distribute one unit to each student and direct students' attention to the Unit Focus and Lesson Checklist. Tell them they will be able to refer to the focus of the unit as needed while working on the lessons. Instruct students to check off each task on the checklist after they complete it.

Read aloud the focus statements, and verify that students understand their purpose for reading. Ask:

- *Who are we going to read about?* (Charles Schulz)

- *What are you going to learn about him?* (what he did during his lifetime)

- *What are you going to write based on this biography?* (a sequence paragraph)

CCSS: **W** 3.2, 3.8 **RIT** 3.3, 3.4, 3.5, 3.10

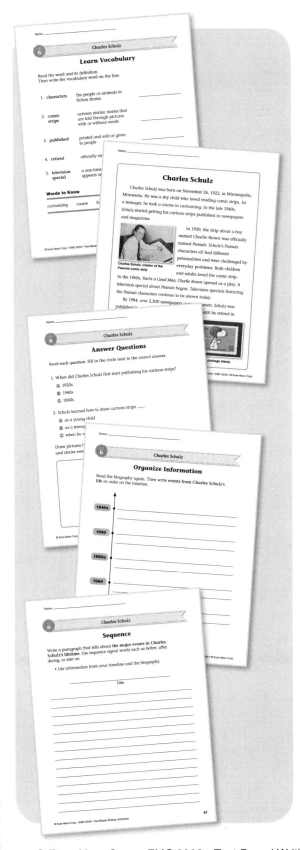

2 Learn Vocabulary

2 Learn Vocabulary

Read aloud each content vocabulary word and have students repeat. Then read aloud and discuss the definitions. Point out that the words are related to Charles Schulz and that students will have a better understanding of the words after they read the biography. Have students write the vocabulary words on the provided lines. Then review the Words to Know, and encourage students to ask questions about any words they do not understand.

3 Read the Biography: *Charles Schulz*

Read aloud the biography as students follow along silently. Then have students reread the biography independently or in small groups.

4 Answer Questions About the Biography

To ensure reading comprehension, have students answer the text-dependent questions. Review the answers together.

5 Organize Information

Explain to students that they will use a timeline graphic organizer to help them plan their paragraphs. Guide students in using the text to complete the organizer, rereading the biography if needed.

Remind students that a sequence paragraph:

• tells the chronological order, or time order, of events, and

• allows readers to understand exactly when events happened.

6 Write a Sequence Paragraph

Instruct students to complete the writing assignment independently, with a partner, or in small groups.

If needed, review the structure of a sequence paragraph:

• The topic sentence introduces the subject.

• Detail sentences support the topic sentence and list events in order.

UNIT
6

Charles Schulz

Unit Focus

You are going to read a biography of Charles Schulz.

As You Read:

Think about what Charles Schulz did in his lifetime.

After You Read:

Use information from the biography to write a sequence paragraph about Charles Schulz's life.

Lesson Checklist

Check off each task after you complete it.

☐ **Learn Vocabulary**

☐ **Read the Biography:** *Charles Schulz*

☐ **Answer Questions About the Biography**

☐ **Organize Information**

☐ **Write a Sequence Paragraph**

Learn Vocabulary

Read the word and its definition.
Then write the vocabulary word on the line.

1. **characters**   the people or animals in fiction stories   _____

2. **comic strips**   cartoon stories; stories that are told through pictures with or without words   _____

3. **published**   printed and sold or given to people   _____

4. **retired**   officially stopped working   _____

5. **television special**   a one-time program that appears on television   _____

Words to Know

cartooning	course	fame	featuring	personalities	teenager

Charles Schulz

Charles Schulz was born on November 26, 1922, in Minneapolis, Minnesota. He was a shy child who loved reading comic strips. As a teenager, he took a course in cartooning. In the late 1940s, Schulz started getting his cartoon strips published in newspapers and magazines.

Charles Schulz, creator of the *Peanuts* comic strip

In 1950, the strip about a boy named Charlie Brown was officially named *Peanuts*. Schulz's *Peanuts* characters all had different personalities and were challenged by everyday problems. Both children and adults loved the comic strip.

In the 1960s, *You're a Good Man, Charlie Brown* opened as a play. A television special about *Peanuts* began. Television specials featuring the *Peanuts* characters continue to be shown today.

By 1984, over 2,300 newspapers carried *Peanuts*. Schulz was published in over 1,400 books. Schulz worked until he retired in 1999. In 2000, Schulz died. He won many awards for his *Peanuts* cartoons and is also in the Cartoonists Hall of Fame. Schulz will always be remembered as one of the greatest cartoonists in the world.

Snoopy U.S. postage stamp

Name _____

 UNIT **6**

Charles Schulz

Answer Questions

Read each question. Fill in the circle next to the correct answer.

1. When did Charles Schulz first start publishing his cartoon strips?

Ⓐ 1920s

Ⓑ 1940s

Ⓒ 1960s

2. Schulz learned how to draw cartoon strips ____.

Ⓐ as a young child

Ⓑ as a teenager

Ⓒ when he retired

Draw pictures that show where Charles Schulz's cartoon strips and stories were published.

Organize Information

Read the biography again. Then write **events from Charles Schulz's life** in order on the timeline.

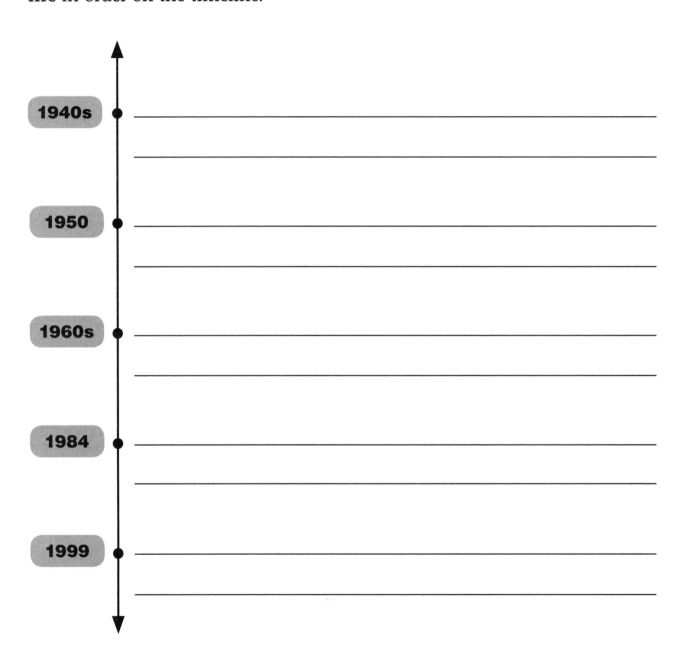

1940s • _____

_____

1950 • _____

_____

1960s • _____

_____

1984 • _____

_____

1999 • _____

_____

Charles Schulz

Sequence

Write a paragraph that tells about **the major events in Charles Schulz's lifetime.** Use sequence signal words such as *before, after, during,* or *later on.*

• Use information from your timeline and the biography.

_____

Title

_____

_____

_____

_____

_____

_____

_____

_____

_____

_____

_____

_____

_____

Pass the Salt

Lesson Objectives

Writing
Students use information from the science article to write an explanatory paragraph.

Vocabulary
Students learn content vocabulary words and use those words to write about salt.

Content Knowledge
Students understand where salt comes from and how it is used.

Essential Understanding
Students understand that animals and humans cannot live without salt.

Prepare

Reproduce and distribute one copy for each student.

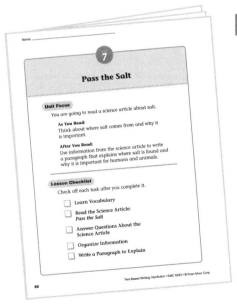

1 Unit Focus and Lesson Checklist
Distribute one unit to each student and direct students' attention to the Unit Focus and Lesson Checklist. Tell them they will be able to refer to the focus of the unit as needed while working on the lessons. Instruct students to check off each task on the checklist after they complete it.

Read aloud the focus statements, and verify that students understand their purpose for reading. Ask:

- *What are we going to read about?* (salt)

- *What are you going to learn about salt?* (where it comes from; why it is important)

- *What are you going to write based on this article?* (a paragraph that explains)

CCSS: **W** 3.2, 3.8 **RIT** 3.3, 3.4, 3.5, 3.10

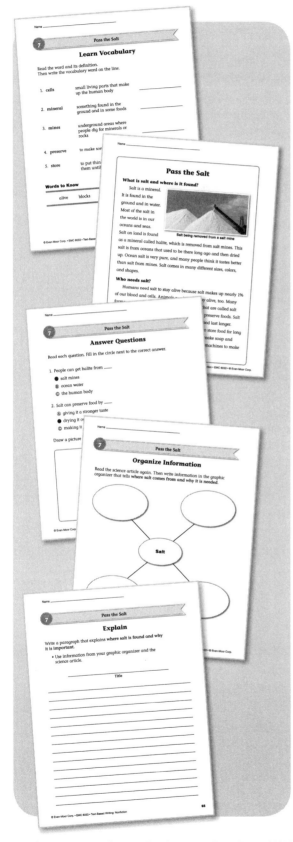

2 Learn Vocabulary

Read aloud each content vocabulary word and have students repeat. Then read aloud and discuss the definitions. Point out that the words are related to salt and that students will have a better understanding of the words after they read the science article. Have students write the vocabulary words on the provided lines. Then review the Words to Know, and encourage students to ask questions about any words they do not understand.

3 Read the Science Article: *Pass the Salt*

Read aloud the science article as students follow along silently. Then have students reread the article independently or in small groups.

4 Answer Questions About the Science Article

To ensure reading comprehension, have students answer the text-dependent questions. Review the answers together.

5 Organize Information

Explain to students that they will use an idea-web organizer to help them plan their paragraphs. Guide students in using the text to complete the organizer, rereading the article if needed.

Remind students that a paragraph that explains:

• gives facts about a topic, and

• tells why or how something is important.

6 Write an Explanatory Paragraph

Instruct students to complete the writing assignment independently, with a partner, or in small groups.

If needed, review the structure of an explanatory paragraph:

• The topic sentence introduces the subject.

• Detail sentences explain the subject to the reader.

UNIT
7

Pass the Salt

Unit Focus

You are going to read a science article about salt.

As You Read:

Think about where salt comes from and why it is important.

After You Read:

Use information from the science article to write a paragraph that explains where salt is found and why it is important for humans and animals.

Lesson Checklist

Check off each task after you complete it.

- [ ] **Learn Vocabulary**

- [ ] **Read the Science Article:** *Pass the Salt*

- [ ] **Answer Questions About the Science Article**

- [ ] **Organize Information**

- [ ] **Write a Paragraph to Explain**

UNIT 7

Pass the Salt

Learn Vocabulary

Read the word and its definition.
Then write the vocabulary word on the line.

1. **cells**   small living parts that make
                 up the human body   _____

2. **mineral**   something found in the
                 ground and in some foods   _____

3. **mines**   underground areas where
                 people dig for minerals or
                 rocks   _____

4. **preserve**   to make something last longer _____

5. **store**   to put things away and keep
                 them until they are needed   _____

Words to Know

alive	blocks	periods	refrigerators	removed

Pass the Salt

What is salt and where is it found?

Salt is a mineral. It is found in the ground and in water. Most of the salt in the world is in our oceans and seas. Salt on land is found

Salt being removed from a salt mine

as a mineral called halite, which is removed from salt mines. This salt is from oceans that used to be there long ago and then dried up. Ocean salt is very pure, and many people think it tastes better than salt from mines. Salt comes in many different sizes, colors, and shapes.

Who needs salt?

Humans need salt to stay alive because salt makes up nearly 1% of our blood and cells. Animals need salt to stay alive, too. Many farmers give their animals large blocks of salt that are called salt licks. Salt is also important because we use it to preserve foods. Salt dries out the food and kills germs, making the food last longer. Before refrigerators were used, people were able to store food for long periods of time by using salt. Salt is also used to make soap and other items. One kind of salt is used in ice-cream machines to make ice cream.

Answer Questions

Read each question. Fill in the circle next to the correct answer.

1. People can get halite from ___.

   Ⓐ salt mines

   Ⓑ ocean water

   Ⓒ the human body

2. Salt can preserve food by ___.

   Ⓐ giving it a stronger taste

   Ⓑ drying it out

   Ⓒ making it more pure

Draw a picture of something that you would need salt to make.

Organize Information

Read the science article again. Then write information in the graphic organizer that tells **where salt comes from and why it is needed**.

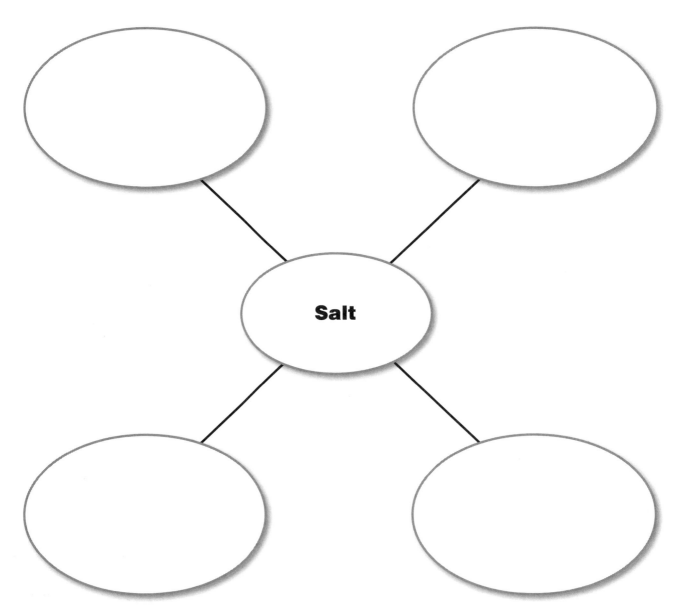

Salt

Explain

Write a paragraph that explains **where salt is found and why it is important**.

- Use information from your graphic organizer and the science article.

_____

Title

_____

_____

_____

_____

_____

_____

_____

_____

_____

_____

_____

The Size of Asia

Lesson Objectives

Writing
Students use information from the social studies article to write an explanatory paragraph.

Vocabulary
Students learn content vocabulary words and use those words to write about Asia's population.

Content Knowledge
Students understand that Asia has grown extensively in the past and probably will continue to do so in the future.

Essential Understanding
Students understand that Asia is, and will continue to be, Earth's most populous continent.

Prepare

Reproduce and distribute one copy for each student.

1 Unit Focus and Lesson Checklist

Distribute one unit to each student and direct students' attention to the Unit Focus and Lesson Checklist. Tell them they will be able to refer to the focus of the unit as needed while working on the lessons. Instruct students to check off each task on the checklist after they complete it.

Read aloud the focus statements, and verify that students understand their purpose for reading. Ask:

- *What are we going to read about?* (the size and population of Asia)

- *What are you going to learn about Asia?* (how it has grown and how it will grow in the future)

- *What are you going to write based on this article?* (a paragraph that explains)

CCSS: **W** 3.2, 3.8   **RIT** 3.3, 3.4, 3.5, 3.10

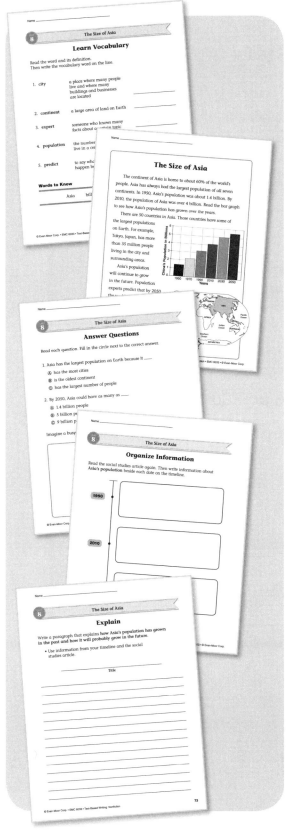

2 Learn Vocabulary

Read aloud each content vocabulary word and have students repeat. Then read aloud and discuss the definitions. Point out that the words are related to Asia's population and that students will have a better understanding of the words after they read the social studies article. Have students write the vocabulary words on the provided lines. Then review the Words to Know, and encourage students to ask questions about any words they do not understand.

3 Read the Social Studies Article: *The Size of Asia*

Read aloud the social studies article as students follow along silently. Then have students reread the article independently or in small groups.

4 Answer Questions About the Social Studies Article

To ensure reading comprehension, have students answer the text-dependent questions. Review the answers together.

5 Organize Information

Explain to students that they will use a timeline graphic organizer to help them plan their paragraphs. Guide students in using the text to complete the organizer, rereading the article if needed.

Remind students that a paragraph that explains:

• tells readers information about a topic, and

• includes facts or predictions about the topic.

6 Write an Explanatory Paragraph

Instruct students to complete the writing assignment independently, with a partner, or in small groups.

If needed, review the structure of an explanatory paragraph:

• The topic sentence introduces the subject.

• Detail sentences explain the subject to the reader.

UNIT
8

The Size of Asia

Unit Focus

You are going to read a social studies article about the size and population of Asia.

As You Read:

Think about how Asia's population has grown over time. Also think about how it will probably grow in the future.

After You Read:

Use information from the article to write a paragraph that explains Asia's past and future populations.

Lesson Checklist

Check off each task after you complete it.

☐ **Learn Vocabulary**

☐ **Read the Social Studies Article:** *The Size of Asia*

☐ **Answer Questions About the Social Studies Article**

☐ **Organize Information**

☐ **Write a Paragraph to Explain**

UNIT 8

The Size of Asia

Learn Vocabulary

Read the word and its definition.
Then write the vocabulary word on the line.

1. **city**   a place where many people
                       live and where many
                       buildings and businesses
                       are located   _____

2. **continent**   a large area of land on Earth   _____

3. **expert**   someone who knows many
                       facts about a certain topic   _____

4. **population**   the number of people who
                       live in a certain area   _____

5. **predict**   to say what is going to
                       happen before it happens   _____

Words to Know

Asia   billion   future   surrounding

The Size of Asia

The continent of Asia is home to about 60% of the world's people. Asia has always had the largest population of all seven continents. In 1950, Asia's population was about 1.4 billion. By 2010, the population of Asia was over 4 billion. Read the bar graph to see how Asia's population has grown over the years.

There are 50 countries in Asia. Those countries have some of the largest populations on Earth. For example, Tokyo, Japan, has more than 35 million people living in the city and surrounding areas.

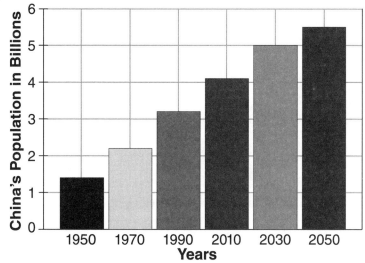

Asia's population will continue to grow in the future. Population experts predict that by 2050, the world will have about 9 billion people, and 5 billion of them will be living in Asia! Asia will keep its place as the largest continent in both size and population for a very long time.

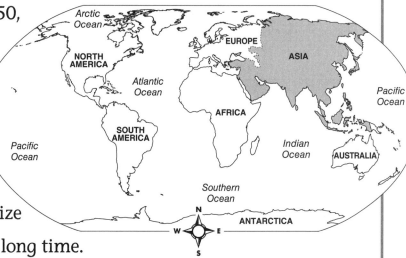

Name _____

Answer Questions

Read each question. Fill in the circle next to the correct answer.

1. Asia has the largest population on Earth because it ____.

   Ⓐ has the most cities

   Ⓑ is the oldest continent

   Ⓒ has the largest number of people

2. By 2050, Asia could have as many as ____.

   Ⓐ 1.4 billion people

   Ⓑ 5 billion people

   Ⓒ 9 billion people

Imagine a busy street somewhere in Asia. Draw what it looks like.

Name _____

The Size of Asia

Organize Information

Read the social studies article again. Then write information about **Asia's population** beside each date on the timeline.

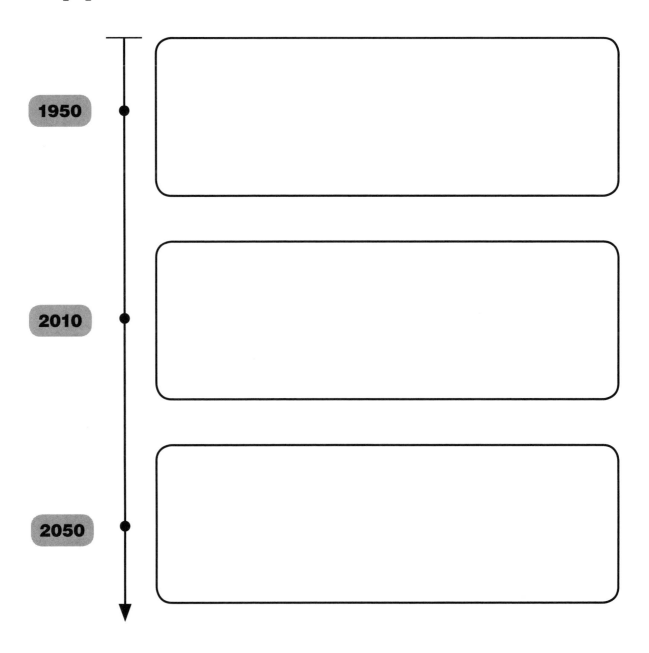

1950

2010

2050

UNIT 8

The Size of Asia

Explain

Write a paragraph that explains **how Asia's population has grown in the past and how it will probably grow in the future.**

- Use information from your timeline and the social studies article.

_____
Title

_____

_____

_____

_____

_____

_____

_____

_____

_____

_____

_____

_____

Birds Migrate

Lesson Objectives

Writing

Students use information from the science article to write a cause-and-effect paragraph.

Vocabulary

Students learn content vocabulary words and use those words to write about why birds migrate.

Content Knowledge

Students understand that birds migrate in the fall and spring in order to find food and protect their young.

Essential Understanding

Students understand that there are good reasons for animals' migrations.

Prepare

Reproduce and distribute one copy for each student.

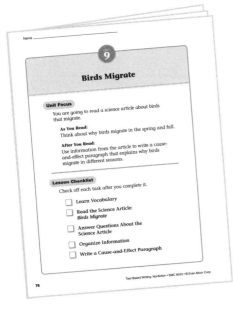

1 Unit Focus and Lesson Checklist

Distribute one unit to each student and direct students' attention to the Unit Focus and Lesson Checklist. Tell them they will be able to refer to the focus of the unit as needed while working on the lessons. Instruct students to check off each task on the checklist after they complete it.

Read aloud the focus statements, and verify that students understand their purpose for reading. Ask:

- *What are we going to read about?* (birds that migrate)

- *What are you going to learn about them?* (why they migrate)

- *What are you going to write based on this article?* (a cause-and-effect paragraph)

CCSS: **W** 3.2, 3.8   **RIT** 3.3, 3.4, 3.5, 3.10

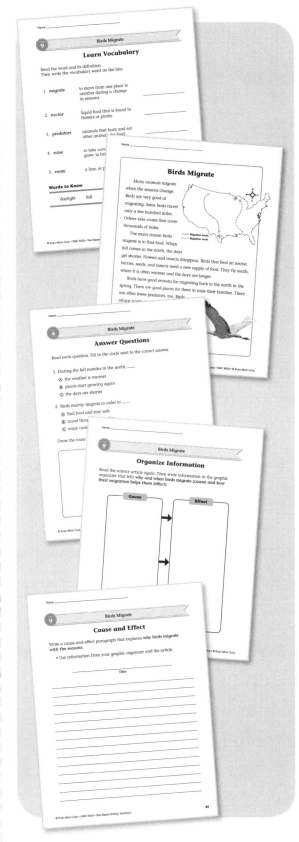

2 Learn Vocabulary

Read aloud each content vocabulary word and have students repeat. Then read aloud and discuss the definitions. Point out that the words are related to bird migration and that students will have a better understanding of the words after they read the science article. Have students write the vocabulary words on the provided lines. Then review the Words to Know, and encourage students to ask questions about any words they do not understand.

3 Read the Science Article: *Birds Migrate*

Read aloud the science article as students follow along silently. Then have students reread the article independently or in small groups.

4 Answer Questions About the Science Article

To ensure reading comprehension, have students answer the text-dependent questions. Review the answers together.

5 Organize Information

Explain to students that they will use a cause-and-effect graphic organizer to help them plan their paragraphs. Guide students in using the text to complete the organizer, rereading the article if needed.

Remind students that a cause-and-effect paragraph:

- tells what happens (effect), and

- tells why it happens (cause).

6 Write a Cause-and-Effect Paragraph

Instruct students to complete the writing assignment independently, with a partner, or in small groups.

If needed, review the structure of a cause-and-effect paragraph:

- The topic sentence tells the cause-and-effect relationship.

- Details support the topic sentence and tell more about the causes and the effects.

UNIT 9

Birds Migrate

Unit Focus

You are going to read a science article about birds that migrate.

As You Read:

Think about why birds migrate in the spring and fall.

After You Read:

Use information from the article to write a cause-and-effect paragraph that explains why birds migrate in different seasons.

Lesson Checklist

Check off each task after you complete it.

- [ ] **Learn Vocabulary**
- [ ] **Read the Science Article:** *Birds Migrate*
- [ ] **Answer Questions About the Science Article**
- [ ] **Organize Information**
- [ ] **Write a Cause-and-Effect Paragraph**

Learn Vocabulary

Read the word and its definition.
Then write the vocabulary word on the line.

1. **migrate**   to move from one place to
                    another during a change
                    in seasons   _____

2. **nectar**   liquid food that is found in
                    flowers or plants   _____

3. **predators**   animals that hunt and eat
                    other animals for food   _____

4. **raise**   to take care of and help to
                    grow; to bring up   _____

5. **route**   a line, or path, of travel   _____

Words to Know

daylight   fall   miles   seasons   spring   travel

Birds Migrate

Many animals migrate when the seasons change. Birds are very good at migrating. Some birds travel only a few hundred miles. Others take routes that cover thousands of miles.

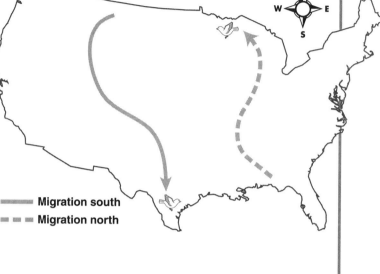

Migration south
Migration north

The main reason birds migrate is to find food. When fall comes in the north, the days get shorter. Flowers and insects disappear. Birds that feed on nectar, berries, seeds, and insects need a new supply of food. They fly south, where it is often warmer and the days are longer.

Birds have good reasons for migrating back to the north in the spring. There are good places for them to raise their families. There are often fewer predators, too. Birds return north during the spring because plants start growing again. There are more hours of daylight during the summer months. This means there's more time to find food. In the fall, the migration will start all over again.

Text-Based Writing: Nonfiction • EMC 6033 • © Evan-Moor Corp.

Birds Migrate

Answer Questions

Read each question. Fill in the circle next to the correct answer.

1. During the fall months in the north, ____.

    Ⓐ the weather is warmer

    Ⓑ plants start growing again

    Ⓒ the days are shorter

2. Birds mainly migrate in order to ____.

    Ⓐ find food and stay safe

    Ⓑ travel thousands of miles

    Ⓒ enjoy cooler weather

Draw the route of a bird flying from north to south during the fall.

Organize Information

Read the science article again. Then write information in the graphic organizer that tells **why and when birds migrate (cause) and how their migration helps them (effect)**.

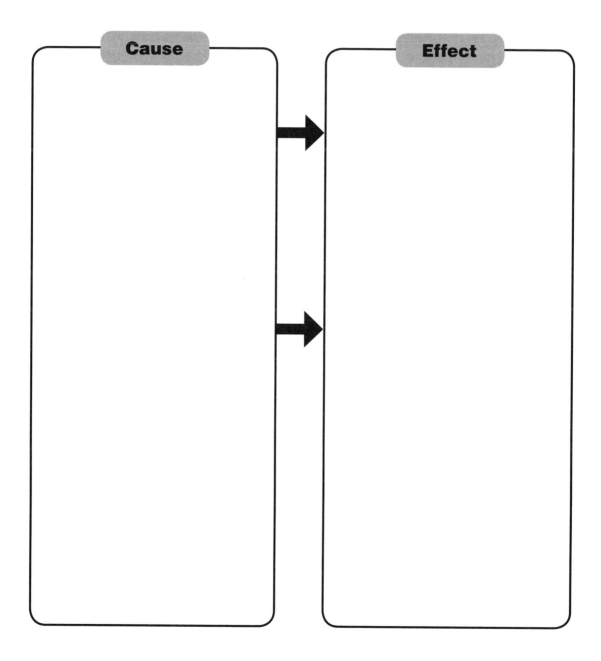

Cause

Effect

Cause and Effect

Write a cause-and-effect paragraph that explains **why birds migrate with the seasons.**

- Use information from your graphic organizer and the article.

_____

Title

_____

_____

_____

_____

_____

_____

_____

_____

_____

_____

Weather Tools

Lesson Objectives

Writing
Students use information from the science article to write an explanatory paragraph.

Vocabulary
Students learn content vocabulary words and use those words to write about weather-related tools.

Content Knowledge
Students understand and can explain the tools that meteorologists use to study wind.

Essential Understanding
Students understand that measuring the wind helps meteorologists keep people safe.

Prepare

Reproduce and distribute one copy for each student.

1 Unit Focus and Lesson Checklist

Distribute one unit to each student and direct students' attention to the Unit Focus and Lesson Checklist. Tell them they will be able to refer to the focus of the unit as needed while working on the lessons. Instruct students to check off each task on the checklist after they complete it.

Read aloud the focus statements, and verify that students understand their purpose for reading. Ask:

• *What are we going to read about?* (wind-measuring tools)

• *What are you going to learn about them?* (how they work; why they're used)

• *What are you going to write based on this article?* (a paragraph that explains)

CCSS: **W** 3.2, 3.8   **RIT** 3.3, 3.4, 3.5, 3.10

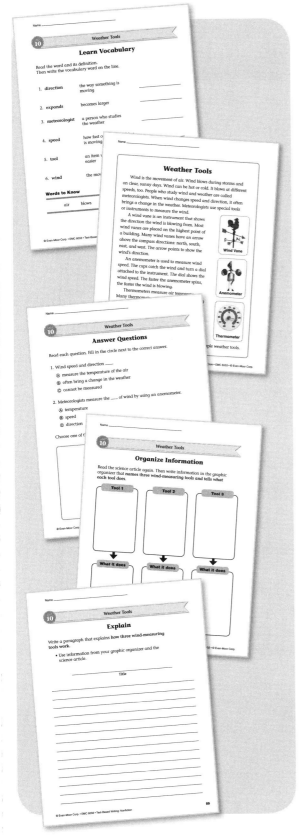

2 Learn Vocabulary

Read aloud each content vocabulary word and have students repeat. Then read aloud and discuss the definitions. Point out that the words are related to wind and that students will have a better understanding of them after they read the science article. Have students write the vocabulary words on the provided lines. Then review the Words to Know, and encourage students to ask questions about any words they do not understand.

3 Read the Science Article: *Weather Tools*

Read aloud the science article as students follow along silently. Then have students reread the article independently or in small groups.

4 Answer Questions About the Science Article

To ensure reading comprehension, have students answer the text-dependent questions. Review the answers together.

5 Organize Information

Explain to students that they will use a graphic organizer to help them plan their paragraphs. Guide students in using the text to complete the organizer, rereading the article if needed.

Remind students that a paragraph that explains:

• tells what something is, and

• tells what something is used for or how it works.

6 Write an Explanatory Paragraph

Instruct students to complete the writing assignment independently, with a partner, or in small groups.

If needed, review the structure of an explanatory paragraph:

• The topic sentence introduces the subject.

• Detail sentences explain the subject to the reader.

UNIT
10

Weather Tools

Unit Focus

You are going to read a science article about tools that are used to measure wind.

As You Read:

Think about what the tools do and why they are used.

After You Read:

Use information from the article to write a paragraph that explains how these tools work.

Lesson Checklist

Check off each task after you complete it.

☐ **Learn Vocabulary**

☐ **Read the Science Article:** *Weather Tools*

☐ **Answer Questions About the Science Article**

☐ **Organize Information**

☐ **Write a Paragraph to Explain**

Learn Vocabulary

Read the word and its definition.
Then write the vocabulary word on the line.

1. **direction**   the way something is
                      moving   _____

2. **expands**   becomes larger   _____

3. **meteorologist** a person who studies
                      the weather   _____

4. **speed**   how fast or slow something
                      is moving   _____

5. **tool**   an item used to make work
                      easier   _____

6. **wind**   the movement of the air   _____

Words to Know

air   blows   measure   spins   temperature

Weather Tools

Wind is the movement of air. Wind blows during storms and on clear, sunny days. Wind can be hot or cold. It blows at different speeds, too. People who study wind and weather are called meteorologists. When wind changes speed and direction, it often brings a change in the weather. Meteorologists use special tools or instruments to measure the wind.

Wind Vane

A wind vane is an instrument that shows the direction the wind is blowing from. Most wind vanes are placed on the highest point of a building. Many wind vanes have an arrow above the compass directions: north, south, east, and west. The arrow points to show the wind's direction.

An anemometer is used to measure wind speed. The cups catch the wind and turn a dial attached to the instrument. The dial shows the wind speed. The faster the anemometer spins, the faster the wind is blowing.

Anemometer

Thermometers measure air temperature. Many thermometers are glass tubes containing a liquid that shows a change in temperature. When air around the tube heats the liquid, the liquid expands and moves up the tube. A scale then shows what the actual air temperature is.

Thermometer

Without these tools, it would be difficult to measure wind. Meteorologists are able to warn people about dangerous storms by using these simple weather tools.

   Text-Based Writing: Nonfiction • EMC 6033 • © Evan-Moor Corp.

Answer Questions

Read each question. Fill in the circle next to the correct answer.

1. Wind speed and direction _____.

   Ⓐ measure the temperature of the air

   Ⓑ often bring a change in the weather

   Ⓒ cannot be measured

2. Meteorologists measure the _____ of wind by using an anemometer.

   Ⓐ temperature

   Ⓑ speed

   Ⓒ direction

Choose one of the weather tools from the article. Draw and label it.

Organize Information

Read the science article again. Then write information in the graphic organizer that **names three wind-measuring tools and tells what each tool does.**

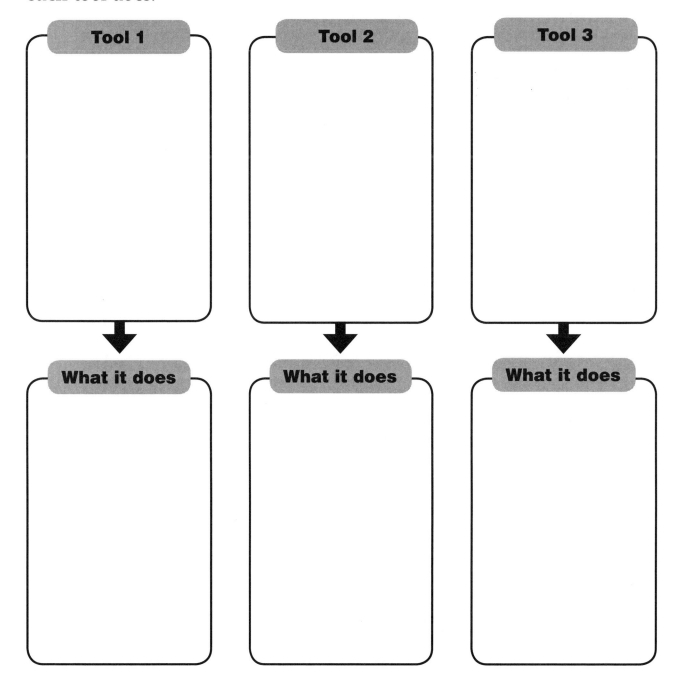

Tool 1	Tool 2	Tool 3
What it does	What it does	What it does

Name _____

Explain

Write a paragraph that explains **how three wind-measuring tools work.**

- Use information from your graphic organizer and the science article.

_____

Title

_____

_____

_____

_____

_____

_____

_____

_____

_____

_____

_____

_____

We Need Sleep

Lesson Objectives

Writing
Students use information from the health article to write a cause-and-effect paragraph.

Vocabulary
Students learn content vocabulary words and use those words to write about sleep.

Content Knowledge
Students understand that humans need sleep to keep their bodies and minds healthy.

Essential Understanding
Students understand that getting enough sleep is an essential part of healthy living.

Prepare

Reproduce and distribute one copy for each student.

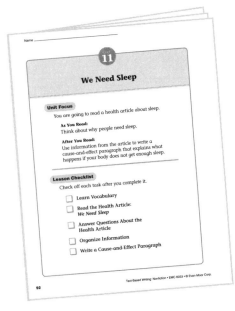

1 Unit Focus and Lesson Checklist

Distribute one unit to each student and direct students' attention to the Unit Focus and Lesson Checklist. Tell them they will be able to refer to the focus of the unit as needed while working on the lessons. Instruct students to check off each task on the checklist after they complete it.

Read aloud the focus statements, and verify that students understand their purpose for reading. Ask:

- *What are we going to read about?* (sleep)

- *What are you going to learn about sleep?* (why we need it)

- *What are you going to write based on this article?* (a cause-and-effect paragraph)

CCSS: **W** 3.2, 3.8   **RIT** 3.3, 3.4, 3.5, 3.10

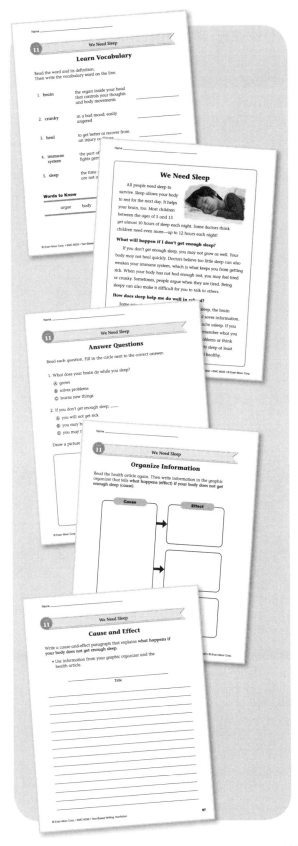

2 Learn Vocabulary

Read aloud each content vocabulary word and have students repeat. Then read aloud and discuss the definitions. Point out that the words are related to sleep and that students will have a better understanding of the words after they read the health article. Have students write the vocabulary words on the provided lines. Then review the Words to Know, and encourage students to ask questions about any words they do not understand.

3 Read the Health Article: *We Need Sleep*

Read aloud the health article as students follow along silently. Then have students reread the article independently or in small groups.

4 Answer Questions About the Health Article

To ensure reading comprehension, have students answer the text-dependent questions. Review the answers together.

5 Organize Information

Explain to students that they will use a cause-and-effect graphic organizer to help them plan their paragraphs. Guide students in using the text to complete the organizer, rereading the article if needed.

Remind students that a cause-and-effect paragraph:

- tells what happens (effect), and
- tells why it happens (cause).

6 Write a Cause-and-Effect Paragraph

Instruct students to complete the writing assignment independently, with a partner, or in small groups.

If needed, review the structure of a cause-and-effect paragraph:

- The topic sentence tells the cause-and-effect relationship.
- Details support the topic sentence and tell more about the causes and the effects.

UNIT
11

We Need Sleep

Unit Focus

You are going to read a health article about sleep.

As You Read:

Think about why people need sleep.

After You Read:

Use information from the article to write a cause-and-effect paragraph that explains what happens if your body does not get enough sleep.

Lesson Checklist

Check off each task after you complete it.

☐ **Learn Vocabulary**

☐ **Read the Health Article:** *We Need Sleep*

☐ **Answer Questions About the Health Article**

☐ **Organize Information**

☐ **Write a Cause-and-Effect Paragraph**

Learn Vocabulary

Read the word and its definition.
Then write the vocabulary word on the line.

1. **brain**   the organ inside your head
                that controls your thoughts
                and body movements   _____

2. **cranky**   in a bad mood; easily
                angered   _____

3. **heal**   to get better or recover from
                an injury or illness   _____

4. **immune**   the part of the body that
   system   fights germs and diseases   _____

5. **sleep**   the time period when you
                are not awake   _____

Words to Know

argue	body	ideas	rest	solves	tired

We Need Sleep

All people need sleep to survive. Sleep allows your body to rest for the next day. It helps your brain, too. Most children between the ages of 5 and 13 get almost 10 hours of sleep each night. Some doctors think children need even more—up to 12 hours each night!

What will happen if I don't get enough sleep?

If you don't get enough sleep, you may not grow as well. Your body may not heal quickly. Doctors believe too little sleep can also weaken your immune system, which is what keeps you from getting sick. When your body has not had enough rest, you may feel tired or cranky. Sometimes, people argue when they are tired. Being sleepy can also make it difficult for you to talk to others.

How does sleep help me do well in school?

Some scientists believe that while you are asleep, the brain thinks about what it learned during the day and saves information. They also say the brain solves problems while you're asleep. If you don't get enough sleep, you may not be able to remember what you have learned. It may be more difficult to solve problems or think of new ideas. To do well in school, you should try to sleep at least 10 hours a night to help keep your body and mind healthy.

Answer Questions

Read each question. Fill in the circle next to the correct answer.

1. What does your brain do while you sleep?

    Ⓐ grows

    Ⓑ solves problems

    Ⓒ learns new things

2. If you don't get enough sleep, _____.

    Ⓐ you will not get sick

    Ⓑ you may be hungry

    Ⓒ you may not grow as well

Draw a picture of someone who is not getting enough sleep.

Name _____

We Need Sleep

Organize Information

Read the health article again. Then write information in the graphic organizer that tells **what happens (effect) if your body does not get enough sleep (cause)**.

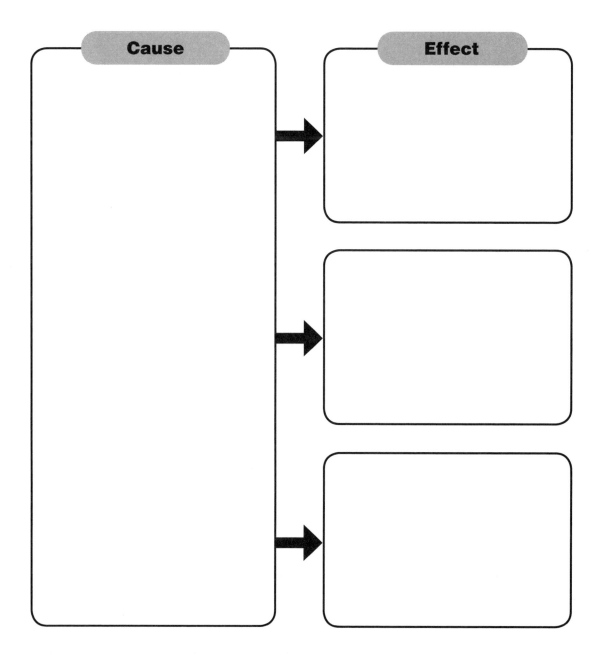

Cause

Effect

Name _____

Cause and Effect

Write a cause-and-effect paragraph that explains **what happens if your body does not get enough sleep**.

- Use information from your graphic organizer and the health article.

_____
Title

_____

_____

_____

_____

_____

_____

_____

_____

_____

_____

_____

Ancient Civilizations

Lesson Objectives

Writing
Students use information from the social studies article to write an opinion paragraph.

Vocabulary
Students learn content vocabulary words and use those words to write about studying ancient civilizations.

Content Knowledge
Students understand that ancient civilizations needed food, water, and shelter to survive.

Essential Understanding
Students understand that ancient civilizations had much in common with today's civilizations.

Prepare

Reproduce and distribute one copy for each student.

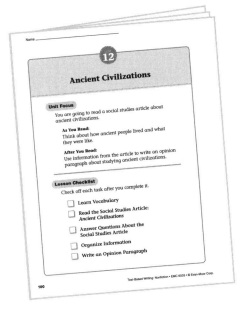

1 Unit Focus and Lesson Checklist

Distribute one unit to each student and direct students' attention to the Unit Focus and Lesson Checklist. Tell them they will be able to refer to the focus of the unit as needed while working on the lessons. Instruct students to check off each task on the checklist after they complete it.

Read aloud the focus statements, and verify that students understand their purpose for reading. Ask:

• *What are we going to read about?* (ancient civilizations)

• *What are you going to learn about them?* (how the people lived)

• *What are you going to write based on this article?* (an opinion paragraph)

CCSS: W 3.1, 3.8   RIT 3.3, 3.4, 3.5, 3.10

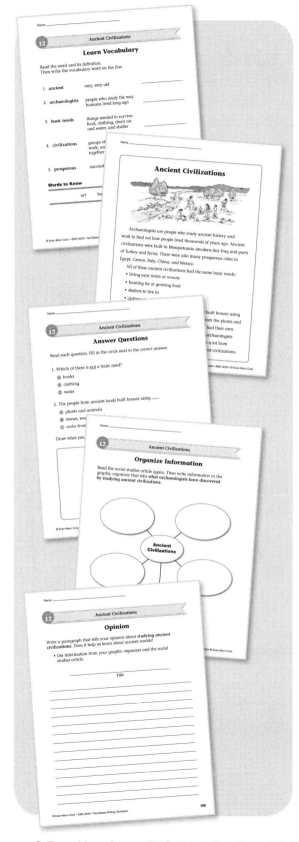

2 Learn Vocabulary

Read aloud each content vocabulary word and have students repeat. Then read aloud and discuss the definitions. Point out that the words are related to ancient civilizations and that students will have a better understanding of the words after they read the social studies article. Have students write the vocabulary words on the provided lines. Then review the Words to Know, and encourage students to ask questions about any words they do not understand.

3 Read the Social Studies Article: *Ancient Civilizations*

Read aloud the social studies article as students follow along silently. Then have students reread the article independently or in small groups.

4 Answer Questions About the Social Studies Article

To ensure reading comprehension, have students answer the text-dependent questions. Review the answers together.

5 Organize Information

Explain to students that they will use an idea-web graphic organizer to help them plan their paragraphs. Guide students in using the text to complete the organizer, rereading the article if needed.

Remind students that an opinion paragraph:

• tells how you feel about something, and

• tells why you feel that way.

6 Write an Opinion Paragraph

Instruct students to complete the writing assignment independently, with a partner, or in small groups.

If needed, review the structure of an opinion paragraph:

• The topic sentence tells your opinion about the subject.

• Detail sentences give reasons that support your opinion.

UNIT
12

Ancient Civilizations

Unit Focus

You are going to read a social studies article about ancient civilizations.

As You Read:

Think about how ancient people lived and what they were like.

After You Read:

Use information from the article to write an opinion paragraph about studying ancient civilizations.

Lesson Checklist

Check off each task after you complete it.

- [ ] **Learn Vocabulary**
- [ ] **Read the Social Studies Article:** *Ancient Civilizations*
- [ ] **Answer Questions About the Social Studies Article**
- [ ] **Organize Information**
- [ ] **Write an Opinion Paragraph**

Learn Vocabulary

Read the word and its definition.
Then write the vocabulary word on the line.

1. **ancient**   very, very old   _____

2. **archaeologists**   people who study the way   _____
                          humans lived long ago

3. **basic needs**   things needed to survive: _____
                          food, clothing, clean air
                          and water, and shelter

4. **civilizations**   groups of people who live,   _____
                          work, and follow rules
                          together

5. **prosperous**   successful or wealthy   _____

Words to Know

art   hunting   religion   shelter

Ancient Civilizations

Archaeologists are people who study ancient history and work to find out how people lived thousands of years ago. Ancient civilizations were built in Mesopotamia (modern-day Iraq and parts of Turkey and Syria). There were also many prosperous cities in Egypt, Greece, Italy, China, and Mexico.

All of these ancient civilizations had the same basic needs:

• living near rivers or oceans

• hunting for or growing food

• shelters to live in

• clothing to wear

The people who lived in these ancient lands built houses using stones, wood, or mud. They wore clothes made from the plants and animals that were in their area. Ancient peoples had their own kinds of art, music, religion, and writing. Today, archaeologists study what these people left behind. We can learn a lot from studying the mistakes and successes of these ancient civilizations.

Answer Questions

Read each question. Fill in the circle next to the correct answer.

1. Which of these is <u>not</u> a basic need?

   Ⓐ books

   Ⓑ clothing

   Ⓒ water

2. The people from ancient lands built houses using ____.

   Ⓐ plants and animals

   Ⓑ stones, wood, or mud

   Ⓒ rocks from rivers and oceans

Draw what you imagine an ancient house might have looked like.

Organize Information

Read the social studies article again. Then write information in the graphic organizer that tells **what archaeologists have discovered by studying ancient civilizations.**

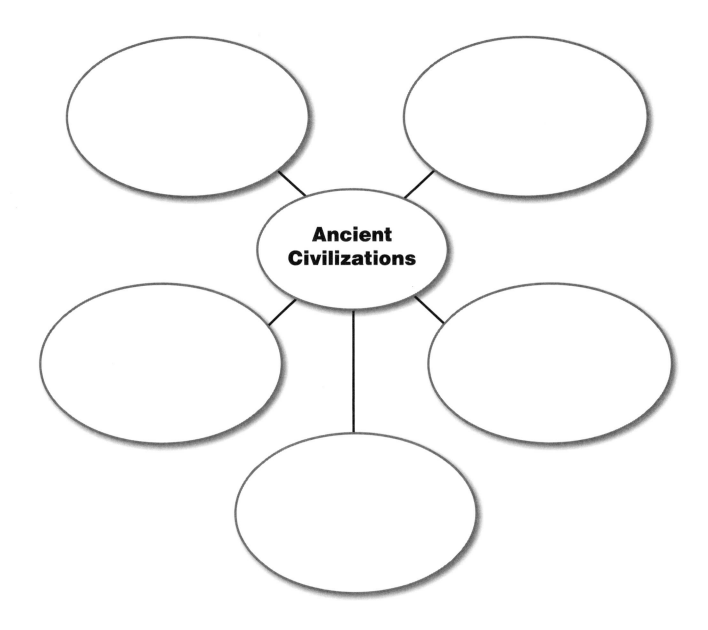

Ancient Civilizations

Opinion

Write a paragraph that tells your opinion about **studying ancient civilizations**. Does it help us learn about ancient worlds?

- Use information from your graphic organizer and the social studies article.

_____
Title

_____

_____

_____

_____

_____

_____

_____

_____

_____

_____

_____

Little Berry, Big Benefit

Lesson Objectives

Writing
Students use information from the health article to write an opinion paragraph.

Vocabulary
Students learn content vocabulary words and use those words to write about blueberries.

Content Knowledge
Students understand that blueberries contain important vitamins and antioxidants.

Essential Understanding
Students understand that people can eat foods such as blueberries to stay healthy and alert.

Prepare

Reproduce and distribute one copy for each student.

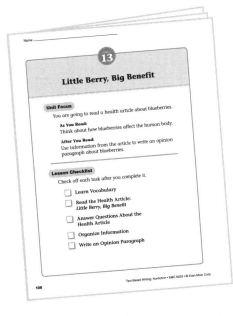

1 Unit Focus and Lesson Checklist

Distribute one unit to each student and direct students' attention to the Unit Focus and Lesson Checklist. Tell them they will be able to refer to the focus of the unit as needed while working on the lessons. Instruct students to check off each task on the checklist after they complete it.

Read aloud the focus statements, and verify that students understand their purpose for reading. Ask:

- *What are we going to read about?* (blueberries)

- *What are you going to learn about them?* (how they affect the body)

- *What are you going to write based on this article?* (an opinion paragraph)

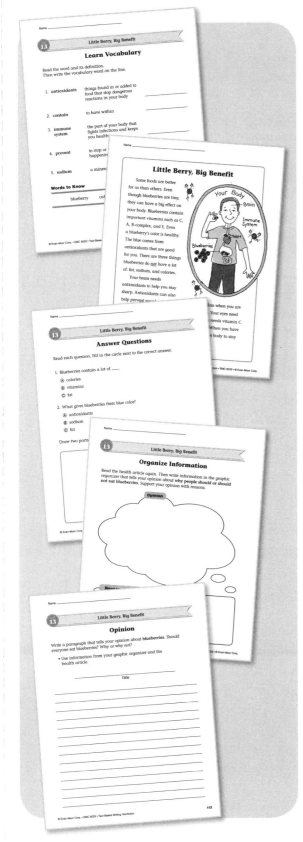

2   Learn Vocabulary

Read aloud each content vocabulary word and have students repeat. Then read aloud and discuss the definitions. Point out that the words are related to blueberries and that students will have a better understanding of the words after they read the health article. Have students write the vocabulary words on the provided lines. Then review the Words to Know, and encourage students to ask questions about any words they do not understand.

3   Read the Health Article: *Little Berry, Big Benefit*

Read aloud the health article as students follow along silently. Then have students reread the article independently or in small groups.

4   Answer Questions About the Health Article

To ensure reading comprehension, have students answer the text-dependent questions. Review the answers together.

5   Organize Information

Explain to students that they will use an opinion graphic organizer to help them plan their paragraphs. Guide students in using the text to complete the organizer, rereading the article if needed.

Remind students that an opinion paragraph:

- tells how you feel about something, and

- tells why you feel that way.

6   Write an Opinion Paragraph

Instruct students to complete the writing assignment independently, with a partner, or in small groups.

If needed, review the structure of an opinion paragraph:

- The topic sentence tells your opinion about the subject.

- Details give reasons why you feel that way.

Little Berry, Big Benefit

Unit Focus

You are going to read a health article about blueberries.

As You Read:

Think about how blueberries affect the human body.

After You Read:

Use information from the article to write an opinion paragraph about blueberries.

Lesson Checklist

Check off each task after you complete it.

- ☐ **Learn Vocabulary**
- ☐ **Read the Health Article:** *Little Berry, Big Benefit*
- ☐ **Answer Questions About the Health Article**
- ☐ **Organize Information**
- ☐ **Write an Opinion Paragraph**

Name _____

Learn Vocabulary

Read the word and its definition.
Then write the vocabulary word on the line.

1. **antioxidants**   things found in or added to food that stop dangerous reactions in your body

    _____

2. **contain**   to have within

    _____

3. **immune system**   the part of your body that fights infections and keeps you healthy

    _____

4. **prevent**   to stop or to keep from happening

    _____

5. **sodium**   a mineral found in table salt   _____

Words to Know

blueberry   calories   memory loss   vitamins

Name _____

Little Berry, Big Benefit

Some foods are better for us than others. Even though blueberries are tiny, they can have a big effect on your body. Blueberries contain important vitamins such as C, A, B-complex, and E. Even a blueberry's color is healthy. The blue comes from antioxidants that are good for you. There are three things blueberries do <u>not</u> have a lot of: fat, sodium, and calories.

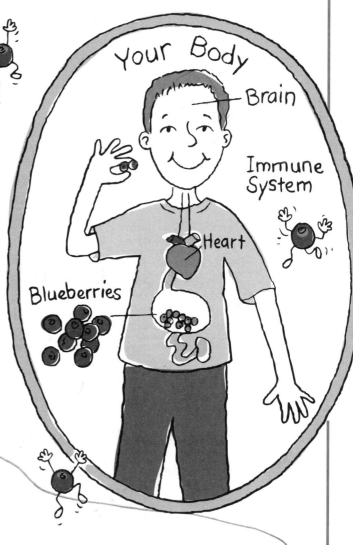

Your brain needs antioxidants to help you stay sharp. Antioxidants can also help prevent your brain from having memory loss when you are much older. Your heart needs antioxidants, too. Your eyes need vitamin A to help you see. Your immune system needs vitamin C and antioxidants to keep you from getting sick. When you have a strong immune system, it's easier for your entire body to stay healthy. Feeling hungry? Eat some blueberries!

110   Text-Based Writing: Nonfiction • EMC 6033 • © Evan-Moor Corp.

Answer Questions

Read each question. Fill in the circle next to the correct answer.

1. Blueberries contain a lot of ___.

   Ⓐ calories

   ● vitamins

   Ⓒ fat

2. What gives blueberries their blue color?

   ● antioxidants

   Ⓑ sodium

   Ⓒ fat

Draw two parts of the body that can be helped by eating blueberries.

UNIT
13

Little Berry, Big Benefit

Organize Information

Read the health article again. Then write information in the graphic organizer that tells your opinion about **why people should or should not eat blueberries**. Support your opinion with reasons.

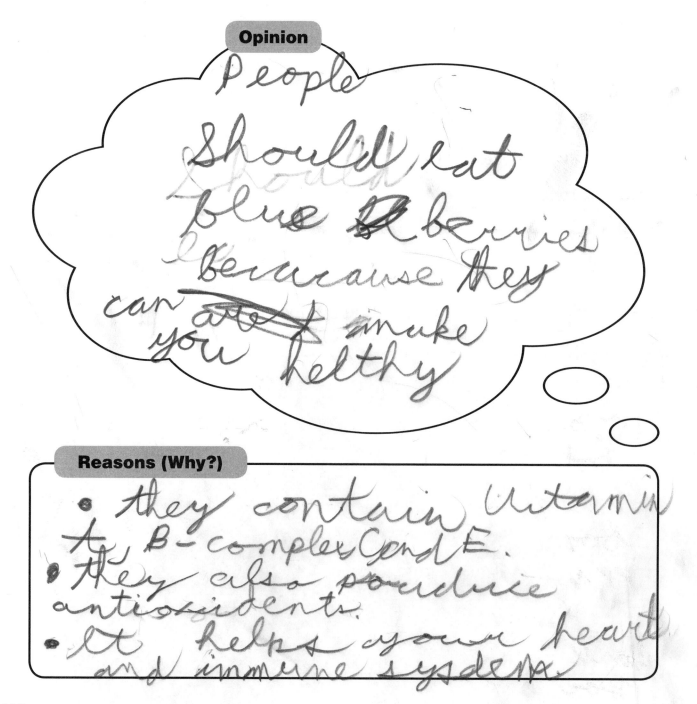

Opinion

People Should eat blue berries beccause they can make you helthy

Reasons (Why?)

- they contain Vitamin A, B-complex C and E.
- they also produce antioxidents.
- It helps your heart and immune system.

Text-Based Writing: Nonfiction • EMC 6033 • © Evan-Moor Corp.

Opinion

Write a paragraph that tells your opinion about **blueberries**. Should everyone eat blueberries? Why or why not?

- Use information from your graphic organizer and the *healthy* health article.

Eat Those Berries!

Title

① I think people should eat blueberries because they can make you helthy. For instance, they contain vitamin A B-complex, C and E. Also they produce antioxidents. Thus I encurage you to eat blueberries! ② Antioxidents and Vitamins help your body in many ways. For exsample, Vitamin C helps your imune system so you don't get sick and Vitamin helps you see. Also, antioxidents help prevent memory loss and they are good for your heart stay healthy too.

John Glenn

Lesson Objectives

Writing
Students use information from the biography to write an argument paragraph.

Vocabulary
Students learn content vocabulary words and use those words to write about why John Glenn is or is not an American hero.

Content Knowledge
Students understand that John Glenn worked for the United States in multiple ways.

Essential Understanding
Students understand that people such as John Glenn inspire others.

Prepare

Reproduce and distribute one copy for each student.

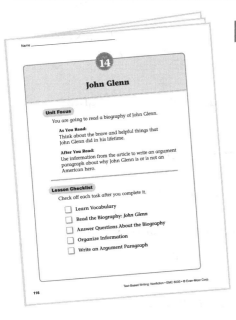

1 Unit Focus and Lesson Checklist

Distribute one unit to each student and direct students' attention to the Unit Focus and Lesson Checklist. Tell them they will be able to refer to the focus of the unit as needed while working on the lessons. Instruct students to check off each task on the checklist after they complete it.

Read aloud the focus statements, and verify that students understand their purpose for reading. Ask:

- *Who are we going to read about?* (John Glenn)

- *What are you going to learn about him?* (his brave and helpful work)

- *What are you going to write based on this biography?* (an argument paragraph)

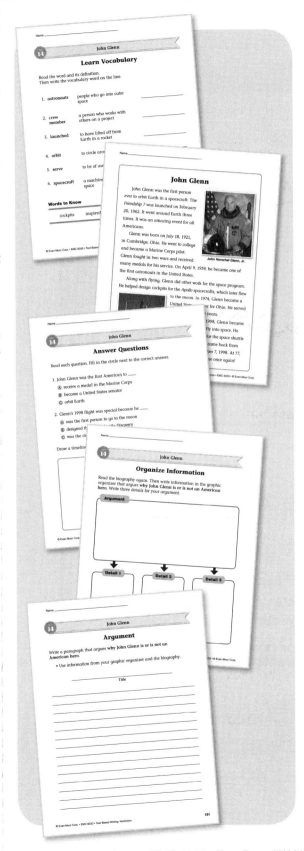

2 **Learn Vocabulary**

Read aloud each content vocabulary word and have students repeat. Then read aloud and discuss the definitions. Point out that the words are related to John Glenn's life and that students will have a better understanding of the words after they read the biography. Have students write the vocabulary words on the provided lines. Then review the Words to Know, and encourage students to ask questions about any words they do not understand.

3 **Read the Biography: *John Glenn***

Read aloud the biography as students follow along silently. Then have students reread the biography independently or in small groups.

4 **Answer Questions About the Biography**

To ensure reading comprehension, have students answer the text-dependent questions. Review the answers together.

5 **Organize Information**

Explain to students that they will use an argument graphic organizer to help them plan their paragraphs. Guide students in using the text to complete the organizer, rereading the biography if needed.

Remind students that an argument paragraph:

- makes an argument for or against something, and

- gives reasons or facts to support the argument.

6 **Write an Argument Paragraph**

Instruct students to complete the writing assignment independently, with a partner, or in small groups.

If needed, review the structure of an argument paragraph:

- The topic sentence states your argument.

- Detail sentences provide examples or reasons that support your argument.

UNIT
14

John Glenn

Unit Focus

You are going to read a biography of John Glenn.

As You Read:

Think about the brave and helpful things that John Glenn did in his lifetime.

After You Read:

Use information from the article to write an argument paragraph about why John Glenn is or is not an American hero.

Lesson Checklist

Check off each task after you complete it.

- [ ] **Learn Vocabulary**
- [ ] **Read the Biography:** *John Glenn*
- [ ] **Answer Questions About the Biography**
- [ ] **Organize Information**
- [ ] **Write an Argument Paragraph**

Learn Vocabulary

Read the word and its definition.
Then write the vocabulary word on the line.

1. **astronauts**   people who go into outer space   _____

2. **crew member**   a person who works with others on a project   _____

3. **launched**   to have lifted off from Earth in a rocket   _____

4. **orbit**   to circle around an object   _____

5. **serve**   to be of use; to help people   _____

6. **spacecraft**   a machine that can fly into space   _____

Words to Know

cockpits   inspired   Marine Corps   pilot   senator

John Glenn

John Glenn was the first person ever to orbit Earth in a spacecraft. The *Friendship 7* was launched on February 20, 1962. It went around Earth three times. It was an amazing event for all Americans.

John Herschel Glenn, Jr.

Glenn was born on July 18, 1921, in Cambridge, Ohio. He went to college and became a Marine Corps pilot. Glenn fought in two wars and received many medals for his service. On April 9, 1959, he became one of the first astronauts in the United States.

Along with flying, Glenn did other work for the space program. He helped design cockpits for the *Apollo* spacecrafts, which later flew

Space shuttle *Discovery*

to the moon. In 1974, Glenn became a United States senator for Ohio. He served in the Senate for 25 years.

On October 29, 1998, Glenn became the oldest person to fly into space. He was a crew member for the space shuttle *Discovery*. The shuttle came back from its journey on November 7, 1998. At 77, Glenn inspired everyone once again!

Text-Based Writing: Nonfiction • EMC 6033 • © Evan-Moor Corp.

John Glenn

Answer Questions

Read each question. Fill in the circle next to the correct answer.

1. John Glenn was the first American to ____.

   Ⓐ receive a medal in the Marine Corps

   Ⓑ become a United States senator

   Ⓒ orbit Earth

2. Glenn's 1998 flight was special because he ____.

   Ⓐ was the first person to go to the moon

   Ⓑ designed the space shuttle *Discovery*

   Ⓒ was the oldest person to fly into space

Draw a timeline of important events in John Glenn's life.

Name _____

Organize Information

Read the biography again. Then write information in the graphic
organizer that argues **why John Glenn is or is not an American
hero**. Write three details for your argument.

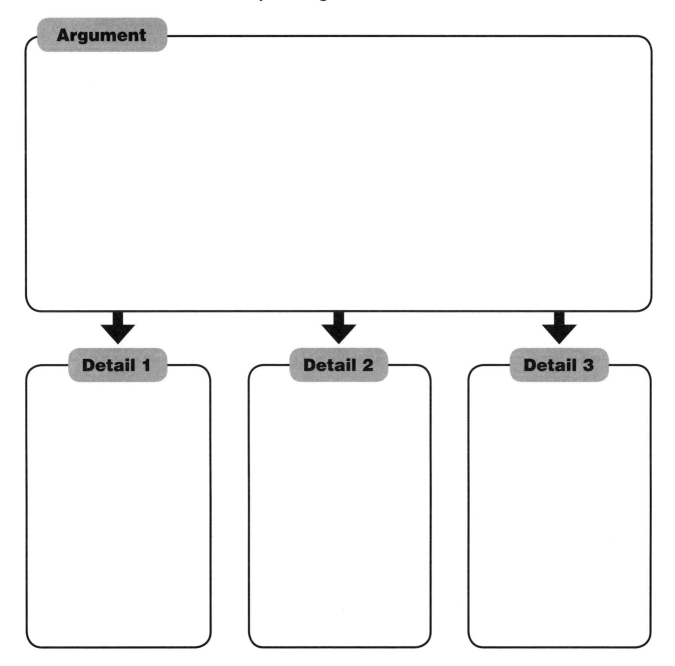

Argument

Detail 1

Detail 2

Detail 3

Name _____

UNIT
14

John Glenn

Argument

Write a paragraph that argues **why John Glenn is or is not an American hero.**

- Use information from your graphic organizer and the biography.

_____

Title

_____

_____

_____

_____

_____

_____

_____

_____

_____

_____

_____

Mexico's Murals

Lesson Objectives

Writing
Students use information from the social studies article to write an argument paragraph.

Vocabulary
Students learn content vocabulary words and use those words to write about Mexico's art murals.

Content Knowledge
Students understand that, after the revolution, the Mexican government wanted to honor its people through art.

Essential Understanding
Students understand that history of all kinds can be preserved and appreciated through art.

Prepare

Reproduce and distribute one copy for each student.

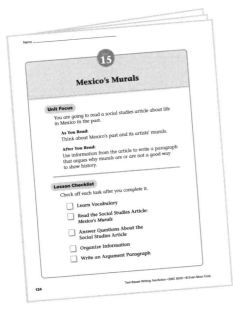

1 Unit Focus and Lesson Checklist

Distribute one unit to each student and direct students' attention to the Unit Focus and Lesson Checklist. Tell them they will be able to refer to the focus of the unit as needed while working on the lessons. Instruct students to check off each task on the checklist after they complete it.

Read aloud the focus statements, and verify that students understand their purpose for reading. Ask:

- *What are we going to read about?* (Mexico)

- *What are you going to learn about it?* (its past; its murals)

- *What are you going to write based on this article?* (an argument paragraph)

CCSS: **W** 3.1, 3.8   **RIT** 3.3, 3.4, 3.5, 3.10

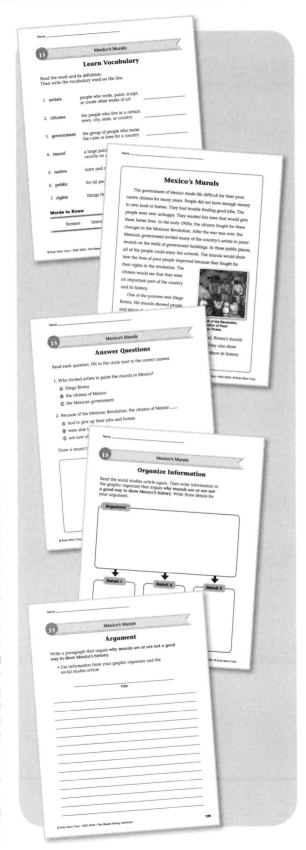

2 Learn Vocabulary

Read aloud each content vocabulary word and have students repeat. Then read aloud and discuss the definitions. Point out that the words are related to Mexico and that students will have a better understanding of the words after they read the social studies article. Have students write the vocabulary words on the provided lines. Then review the Words to Know, and encourage students to ask questions about any words they do not understand.

3 Read the Social Studies Article: *Mexico's Murals*

Read aloud the social studies article as students follow along silently. Then have students reread the article independently or in small groups.

4 Answer Questions About the Social Studies Article

To ensure reading comprehension, have students answer the text-dependent questions. Review the answers together.

5 Organize Information

Explain to students that they will use an argument graphic organizer to help them plan their writing. Guide students in using the text to complete the organizer, rereading the article if needed.

Remind students that an argument paragraph:

• makes an argument for or against something, and

• gives reasons or facts to support the argument.

6 Write an Argument Paragraph

Instruct students to complete the writing assignment independently, with a partner, or in small groups.

If needed, review the structure of an argument paragraph:

• The topic sentence states your argument.

• Detail sentences provide examples or reasons that support your argument.

UNIT
15

Mexico's Murals

Unit Focus

You are going to read a social studies article about life in Mexico in the past.

As You Read:

Think about Mexico's past and its artists' murals.

After You Read:

Use information from the article to write a paragraph that argues why murals are or are not a good way to show history.

Lesson Checklist

Check off each task after you complete it.

☐ **Learn Vocabulary**

☐ **Read the Social Studies Article:** *Mexico's Murals*

☐ **Answer Questions About the Social Studies Article**

☐ **Organize Information**

☐ **Write an Argument Paragraph**

Learn Vocabulary

Read the word and its definition.
Then write the vocabulary word on the line.

1. **artists**   people who write, paint, sculpt,
             or create other works of art   _____

2. **citizens**   the people who live in a certain
             town, city, state, or country   _____

3. **government**   the group of people who make
             the rules or laws for a country   _____

4. **mural**   a large painting or drawing,
             usually on a wall   _____

5. **native**   born and raised in a country   _____

6. **public**   for all people to use or see   _____

7. **rights**   things the law allows you to do _____

Words to Know

farmers   history   past   revolution   workers

Mexico's Murals

The government of Mexico made life difficult for their poor, native citizens for many years. People did not have enough money to own land or homes. They had trouble finding good jobs. The people were very unhappy. They wanted fair laws that would give them better lives. In the early 1900s, the citizens fought for these changes in the Mexican Revolution. After the war was over, the Mexican government invited many of the country's artists to paint murals on the walls of government buildings. In these public places, all of the people could enjoy the artwork. The murals would show how the lives of poor people improved because they fought for their rights in the revolution. The citizens would see that they were an important part of the country and its history.

Triumph of the Revolution, Distribution of Food by Diego Rivera

One of the painters was Diego Rivera. His murals showed people and places during and after the revolution. One mural shows farmers, workers, and their families. They are sharing the food they grew on their own new land. Rivera's murals show important events in the history of Mexico. They also show what life looked like in the past. Mexico's murals share its history with its citizens and with the rest of the world.

Name _____

Answer Questions

Read each question. Fill in the circle next to the correct answer.

1. Who invited artists to paint the murals in Mexico?

   Ⓐ Diego Rivera

   Ⓑ the citizens of Mexico

   Ⓒ the Mexican government

2. Because of the Mexican Revolution, the citizens of Mexico ____.

   Ⓐ had to give up their jobs and homes

   Ⓑ were able to buy land

   Ⓒ are now able to see less art

Draw a mural that shows people before the Mexican Revolution.

Name _____

Organize Information

Read the social studies article again. Then write information in the graphic organizer that argues **why murals are or are not a good way to show Mexico's history**. Write three details for your argument.

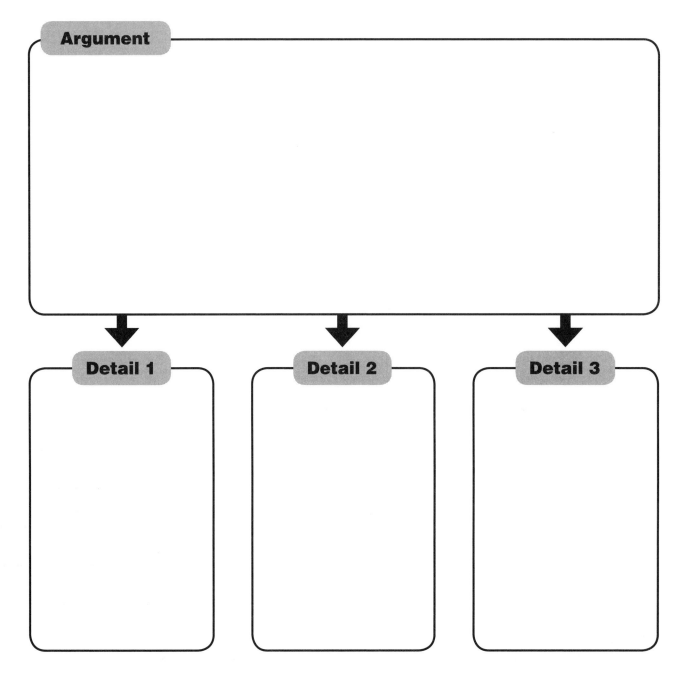

Argument

Detail 1

Detail 2

Detail 3

Mexico's Murals

Argument

Write a paragraph that argues **why murals are or are not a good way to show Mexico's history.**

- Use information from your graphic organizer and the social studies article.

_____

Title

_____

_____

_____

_____

_____

_____

_____

_____

_____

_____

_____

TE = Teacher's Edition
SB = Student Book

Answer Key

Unit 1

TE Page 15 / SB Page 6

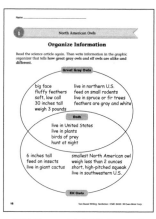
TE Page 16 / SB Page 7

Unit 2
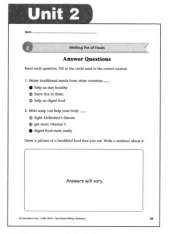
TE Page 23 / SB Page 12

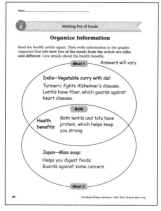
TE Page 24 / SB Page 13

Unit 3

TE Page 31 / SB Page 18

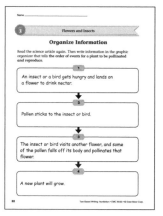
TE Page 32 / SB Page 19

Unit 4
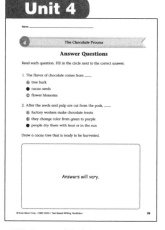
TE Page 39 / SB Page 24

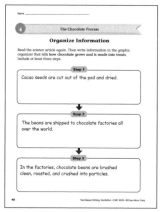
TE Page 40 / SB Page 25

Unit 5

TE Page 47 / SB Page 30

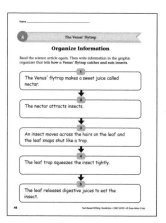
TE Page 48 / SB Page 31

Unit 6

TE Page 55 / SB Page 36

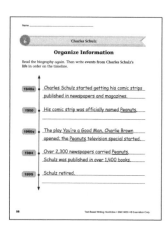
TE Page 56 / SB Page 37

Unit 7

TE Page 63 / SB Page 42

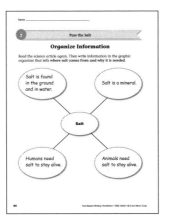

TE Page 64 / SB Page 43

Unit 8

TE Page 71 / SB Page 48

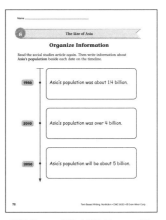

TE Page 72 / SB Page 49

Unit 9

TE Page 79 / SB Page 54

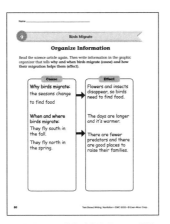

TE Page 80 / SB Page 55

Unit 10

TE Page 87 / SB Page 60

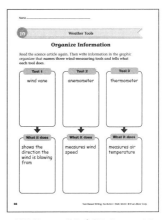

TE Page 88 / SB Page 61

Unit 11

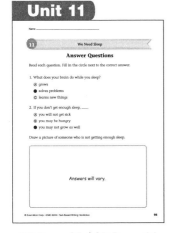

TE Page 95 / SB Page 66

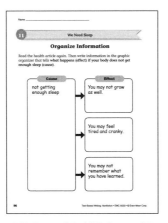

TE Page 96 / SB Page 67

Unit 12

TE Page 103 / SB Page 72

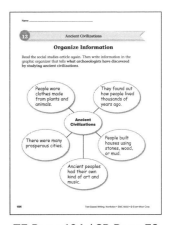

TE Page 104 / SB Page 73

Unit 13

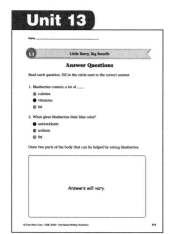

13 Little Berry, Big Benefit

Answer Questions

Read each question. Fill in the circle next to the correct answer.

1. Blueberries contain a lot of ____
   - calories
   - ● vitamins
   - fat

2. What gives blueberries their blue color?
   - ● antioxidants
   - sodium
   - fat

Draw two parts of the body that can be helped by eating blueberries.

Answers will vary.

TE Page 111 / SB Page 78

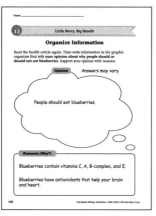

13 Little Berry, Big Benefit

Organize Information

Read the health article again. Then write information in the graphic organizer that tells **your opinion about why people should or should not eat blueberries.** Support your opinion with reasons.

Opinion — Answers may vary.

People should eat blueberries.

Reasons (Why?)

Blueberries contain vitamins C, A, B-complex, and E.

Blueberries have antioxidants that help your brain and heart.

TE Page 112 / SB Page 79

Unit 14

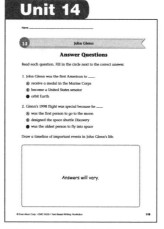

14 John Glenn

Answer Questions

Read each question. Fill in the circle next to the correct answer.

1. John Glenn was the first American to ____
   - ● receive a medal in the Marine Corps
   - become a United States senator
   - orbit Earth

2. Glenn's 1998 flight was special because he ____
   - ● was the first person to go to the moon
   - designed the space shuttle *Discovery*
   - was the oldest person to fly into space

Draw a timeline of important events in John Glenn's life.

Answers will vary.

TE Page 119 / SB Page 84

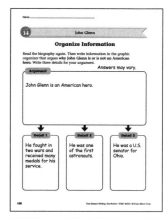

14 John Glenn

Organize Information

Read the biography again. Then write information in the graphic organizer that argues **why John Glenn is or is not an American hero.** Write three details for your argument.

Argument — Answers may vary.

John Glenn is an American hero.

Detail 1	Detail 2	Detail 3
He fought in two wars and received many medals for his service.	He was one of the first astronauts.	He was a U.S. senator for Ohio.

TE Page 120 / SB Page 85

Unit 15

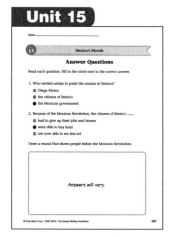

15 Mexico's Murals

Answer Questions

Read each question. Fill in the circle next to the correct answer.

1. Who invited artists to paint the murals in Mexico?
   - Diego Rivera
   - the citizens of Mexico
   - ● the Mexican government

2. Because of the Mexican Revolution, the citizens of Mexico ____
   - had to give up their jobs and homes
   - ● were able to buy land
   - are now able to see less art

Draw a mural that shows people before the Mexican Revolution.

Answers will vary.

TE Page 127 / SB Page 90

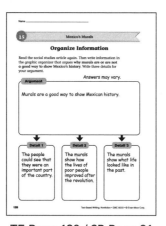

15 Mexico's Murals

Organize Information

Read the social studies article again. Then write information in the graphic organizer that argues **why murals are or are not a good way to show Mexico's history.** Write three details for your argument.

Argument — Answers may vary.

Murals are a good way to show Mexican history.

Detail 1	Detail 2	Detail 3
The people could see that they were an important part of the country.	The murals show how the lives of poor people improved after the revolution.	The murals show what life looked like in the past.

TE Page 128 / SB Page 91

Common Core Lessons

Reading Informational Text

Grade 3

SAMPLER

Science Article
Text Structure: Compare and Contrast

Big, Wild Cats!

Lesson Objective   Students will explain how a tiger moves, eats, and lives in the forests and jungles of Asia.

Content Knowledge   Animals depend on the land, water, and air to live and grow.

Lesson Preparation

Reproduce and distribute one copy of the article, dictionary page, and activity pages to each student.

Big, Wild Cats!

The roar of a lion or a tiger can make a person shake with fear. Lions and tigers are close relatives, but they have differences, too.

Where Lions and Tigers Live

These big cats both live in the wild. However, they live in different parts of the world. Lions live in the grasslands of Africa. Their sandy-colored fur blends in with the tall yellow grasses. Tigers live in forests and jungles in Asia. Their orange fur has dark stripes that help them hide among trees. No two tigers have the same pattern of stripes.

The weather is hot where lions and tigers live. Lions like to stay dry. They go into water only if they have to. However, tigers are good swimmers. They may swim across rivers to hunt. They also go into water to cool off.

How Big Cats Live

Both kinds of big cats live and hunt in an area that covers many miles. This area is their *territory*. Lions live in family groups called *prides*. A pride has males, females, and their cubs. Each pride has its own territory. Lions roar to guard their territory. An adult lion's roar can be heard up to five miles away.

Lions live in family groups called prides.

Unlike lions, tigers do not live in groups. A mother tiger raises her cubs without their father. The cubs stay with their mother for only two years. Then they live alone in their own territory.

Reading Informational Text • EMC 3203 • © Evan-Moor Corp.

14

...and tigers are in danger. Many lions die from sicknesses caused by hot weather and not enough water. Also, lions are losing their territories because people are using the land to grow food. Long ago, lions were found in Africa, Asia, and Europe. Today, they live only in Africa and in one forest in India.

Some people hunt tigers for their skin and other parts. Tigers are losing their territories as forests are cut down. Tigers used to live in many parts of Asia. Today, they live only in small areas. Many people are working to save lions and tigers.

Unlike lions, tigers hunt alone. This tiger is creeping toward its prey.

© Evan-Moor Corp. • EMC 3203 • Reading Informational Text   15

CCSS: **RIT** 3.1, 3.2, 3.3, 3.4, 3.5, 3.7, 3.8   **W** 3.2

1 Read Aloud the Article

Read aloud *Big, Wild Cats!* Have students follow along silently as you read.

2 Introduce the Vocabulary

Content Vocabulary
Read aloud the Content Vocabulary words and definitions. Point out that *grasslands* is a compound word that contains the words *grass* and *lands*. The two words give clues about the meaning of the word. Explain that *sandy-colored* is another compound word used in the article. It is a describing word that has a hyphen connecting its two word parts. Discuss definitions and usage as needed.

Academic Vocabulary
Next, read aloud the Academic Vocabulary words and definitions. Discuss definitions and usage as needed. Then read these context sentences from the article, emphasizing the Academic Vocabulary words:

*Lions and tigers are close **relatives**, but they have differences, too.*

*A pride has **males**, **females**, and their cubs.*

*An **adult** lion's roar can be heard up to five miles away.*

3 Students Read the Article

Have students read the article independently, with a partner, or in small groups. After students read, guide a discussion about the article. Direct students' attention to graphic elements or visual aids.

4 Identify Information

Explain that students will locate important information in the article. After students complete the activity, allow time for a question-and-answer session.

5 Answer Questions

Encourage students to use the article to answer the questions and/or check their answers.

6 Apply Vocabulary

Have students reread the article before they complete the vocabulary activity. Optional: Have students mark each vocabulary word as they read.

7 Examine Text Structure

Read aloud the Compare and Contrast description and Signal Words. Then have students read the article again, underlining signal words in red. Then guide students in completing the activity.

8 Write About It:
A Tiger's Life

Have students complete the writing activity independently or in small groups.

Big, Wild Cats!

The roar of a lion or a tiger can make a person shake with fear. Lions and tigers are close relatives, but they have differences, too.

Where Lions and Tigers Live

These big cats both live in the wild. However, they live in different parts of the world. Lions live in the grasslands of Africa. Their sandy-colored fur blends in with the tall yellow grasses. Tigers live in forests and jungles in Asia. Their orange fur has dark stripes that help them hide among trees. No two tigers have the same pattern of stripes.

The weather is hot where lions and tigers live. Lions like to stay dry. They go into water only if they have to. However, tigers are good swimmers. They may swim across rivers to hunt. They also go into water to cool off.

How Big Cats Live

Both kinds of big cats live and hunt in an area that covers many miles. This area is their *territory*. Lions live in family groups called *prides*. A pride has males, females, and their cubs. Each pride has its own territory. Lions roar to guard their territory. An adult lion's roar can be heard up to five miles away.

Lions live in family groups called prides.

Unlike lions, tigers do not live in groups. A mother tiger raises her cubs without their father. The cubs stay with their mother for only two years. Then they live alone in their own territory.

How Lions and Tigers Catch Their Food

Lions and tigers are meat eaters. Both kinds of cats are strong hunters that have sharp teeth and claws. Lions and tigers both creep up on their prey and attack by surprise. Female lions do most of the hunting. They may work as a team to hunt animals that are faster than they are. Unlike lions, tigers hunt alone.

Dangers to Big Cats

Both lions and tigers are in danger. Many lions die from sicknesses caused by hot weather and not enough water. Also, lions are losing their territories because people are using the land to grow food. Long ago, lions were found in Africa, Asia, and Europe. Today, they live only in Africa and in one forest in India.

Unlike lions, tigers hunt alone. This tiger is creeping toward its prey.

Some people hunt tigers for their skin and other parts. Tigers are losing their territories as forests are cut down. Tigers used to live in many parts of Asia. Today, they live only in small areas. Many people are working to save lions and tigers.

Name: _____

Dictionary

Content Vocabulary

attack
to try to hurt or kill

forests
areas of land where many trees grow

grasslands
areas of land that are covered with grasses but not trees or bushes

jungles
areas of land that are thickly covered with bushes, trees, and vines

prey
animals that are hunted and eaten by other animals

Academic Vocabulary

relatives
members of the same family or animal group

males
animals that can be the father of young

females
animals that can be the mother of young

adult
a full-grown animal

Write a sentence that includes a vocabulary word.

_____

_____

Identify Information

You can understand a text better if you read it more than once. Look for the following information as you read the article again. Put a check mark in the box after you complete each task.

		I did it!
✏️	Highlight any words that describe where lions live.	☐
☐	Draw a box around any words that describe where tigers live.	☐
○	Circle four words that describe the fur of lions and tigers.	☐
—	Draw a line under the sentence that explains how tigers cool off.	☐
[ ]	Put brackets around the sentences that explain what a territory is.	☐
★	Draw a star next to the paragraph about how lions and tigers hunt.	☐
✖	Put an X next to each paragraph that explains why people are working to save lions and tigers.	☐
▲	Draw a triangle next to any information that surprised or interested you.	☐
?	Put a question mark beside any words or sentences you don't understand.	☐

Answer Questions

Use information from the article to answer each question.

1. Lions live in Africa's grasslands, but tigers live in _____.

    Ⓐ Africa's forests

    Ⓑ Asia's grasslands

    Ⓒ Asia's jungles

    Ⓓ Africa and Asia

2. Both lions and tigers have _____.

    Ⓐ prides

    Ⓑ their own territories

    Ⓒ dark stripes

    Ⓓ sandy-colored fur

3. When they hunt, both kinds of big cats _____.

    Ⓐ attack by surprise

    Ⓑ roar loudly

    Ⓒ work as a team

    Ⓓ work alone

4. How does a lion's fur help it live in the wild?

    _____

    _____

5. How does a tiger's fur help it live in the wild?

    _____

    _____

Apply Vocabulary

Use a word from the word box to complete each sentence.

Word Box

females	grasslands	prey
jungles	relatives	males
attack	forests	adult

1. Lions blend in with Africa's _____ because of the color of their fur.

2. Among lions, _____ do most of the hunting.

3. Tigers and lions are both cats, which makes them _____.

4. Animals that live in forests and _____ are food for tigers.

5. A team of female lions may work together to hunt _____.

6. Among tigers, the _____ do not help raise their own cubs.

7. An _____ lion's roar can be heard miles away.

8. Tigers can be found in _____ and jungles throughout Asia.

9. Lions and tigers use sharp teeth and claws to _____ their prey.

Compare and Contrast

A text that has a **compare-and-contrast** structure is about two main ideas. It tells how the two ideas are alike (compares). It also tells how the two ideas are different (contrasts).

Authors use these signal words to create a **compare-and-contrast** structure:

Signal Words		
both	today	but
long ago	however	unlike

1. The first paragraph tells us that the article will compare and contrast what two things?

   _____

2. Write the sentence that tells how tigers are different from lions in the way they live.

   _____

   _____

3. Are lions and tigers alike or different in what they eat? Write the sentence from the article that tells you how they are similar or different.

   _____

   _____

Name: _____

Write About It

Explain how a tiger moves, eats, and lives in the forests and jungles of Asia. Include facts and details from the article.

A Tiger's Life

_____

_____

_____

_____

_____

_____

_____

_____

_____

_____

_____

_____

_____

_____

_____